W9-BSJ-442

PSYCHOLOGICAL
REPORTS
Third Edition

PSYCHOLOGICAL REPORTS

A GUIDE TO REPORT WRITING IN PROFESSIONAL PSYCHOLOGY

Third Edition

Raymond L. Ownby

RECEIVED
JAN 20 1998
MSU - LIBRARY

John Wiley & Sons, Inc.
New York • Chichester • Weinheim • Brisbane • Singapore • Toronto

BF
76.8
.O86
1997

This text is printed on acid-free paper.

Copyright © 1997 by John Wiley & Sons, Inc.

All rights reserved. Published simultaneously in Canada.

Though this book is nonfiction, the names and distinguishing traits of all clients and individuals mentioned in the book have been changed.

Reproduction or translation of any part of this work beyond that permitted by Section 107 or 108 of the 1976 United States Copyright Act without permission of the copyright owner is unlawful. Requests for permission or further information should be addressed to the Permissions Department, John Wiley & Sons, Inc., 605 Third Avenue, New York, NY 10158-0012.

This publication is designed to provide accurate and authoritative information in regard to the subject matter covered. It is sold with the understanding that the publisher is not engaged in rendering professional services. If legal, accounting, medical, psychological, or any other expert assistance is required, the services of a competent professional person should be sought.

Library of Congress Cataloging-in-Publication Data

Ownby, Raymond L.
    Psychological reports : a guide to report writing in professional psychology / by Raymond L. Ownby. — 3rd ed.
        p.   cm.
    Includes bibliographical references and index.
    ISBN 0-471-16887-4 (paper : alk. paper)
    1. Psychology—Authorship.   2. Psychological literature.
3. Report writing.   I. Title.
BF76.8.O86   1997
808'.06615—dc20   96-20539

Printed in the United States of America

10 9 8 7 6 5 4 3 2 1

34710863
1-22-98

PREFACE

In this third edition of *Psychological Reports*, I have once again tried to build on the strengths of earlier editions, making changes to improve the book. This edition has been rewritten throughout to improve its readability and to reflect recent developments in assessment, such as the introduction of the third edition of the Wechsler Intelligence Scale for Children (WISC-III). Illustrative material has been added where needed.

The review of research about reporting in chapter 2 has been updated. Research about reporting continues to appear, and computerized searching has made finding it much easier. The presentation of the expository process model in chapter 4 has been expanded and supplemented with new figures. The series of appendixes added in the second edition has been retained, and the glossary has been expanded. I want to continue to acknowledge the contributions of reviewers of the first edition of *Psychological Reports*: Gilbert Gredler (1987), David Hanson (1988), and Norman Sundberg (1989). Their comments were, in many cases, incorporated in the second edition; most of these changes remain in this edition.

I want to thank the staff of Clinical Psychology Publishing Company for their support and assistance. The staff of John Wiley & Sons—Kelly Franklin and Linda Witzling—and of Pageworks—Maggie Dana and Susan McIntyre—rendered invaluable assistance that is deeply appreciated. Fred Wallbrown at Kent State University was a long-time teacher, mentor, and friend. He died in 1995, and his absence is felt. Fred was interested in report writing, and we collaborated on a number of the studies mentioned in this book. He contributed in many other informal ways to the previous editions of this book, and his continuing influence in this edition deserves acknowledgment.

The continuing acceptance of this book is indeed gratifying. I hope that this third edition will also be useful in helping to improve your report writing.

RAY OWNBY

CONTENTS

Contents

Contents

Contents

LIST OF
ILLUSTRATIONS

1

INTRODUCTION

Assessment is a key professional task for psychologists, and the written report that results is an important part of that task. Surprisingly little attention has been paid to finding out what makes these reports useful and effective. This book's purpose is to give psychologists guidance about the best ways to communicate the results of individual client assessments. Past research on reports can answer some questions about how to write reports, but when research is ambiguous or nonexistent, psychologists must rely on expert opinion.

The dearth of research may be the result of widespread devaluation of assessment activities by psychologists since the 1950s; in recent years, therapeutic activities have been emphasized. It may also be the result of the general neglect of productive written language as a research topic (Britton & Black, 1985, p. 2) and a lack of awareness about how important it is to prepare effective reports. Studies of reporting are published sporadically, and their reference lists often suggest little awareness of previous studies. When the first edition of this book appeared in 1987, *Psychological Abstracts* (an important index for periodicals with psychological content) did not have a heading or key word for reports. If you wanted to find research on reports, you were forced to look under more general topics related to professional practice such as psychometrics or school, clinical, or counseling psychology. Now, the *Thesaurus of Psychological Index Terms* (Walken, 1994) includes the term *psychological reports*. This inclusion greatly simplifies computerized searches for information about reports. Still, a computerized search on this term results in fewer than 25 references, of which only 6 are research studies. Although psychologists have continued to write assessment reports, they have seldom studied the best ways to do so.

An informal review suggests that most psychologists learn about report writing only peripherally in graduate-level assessment courses. They have rarely been specifically taught how to write reports. During training, student psychologists are understandably preoccupied with the mechanics of test administration and scoring, and spend little time learning how to write assessment reports. Instructors rarely have a guide with which to teach students about report writing. Even after formal training in assessment is over, the demands of everyday practice make it hard for psychologists to find the time to examine their report writing critically. As you will see, taking time to reflect on your writing and to ask for reactions from your readers is essential to improving your reports.

Psychologists often find report writing an onerous task, undertaken only under duress. There are many reasons why psychologists do not like to write reports. Report writing is a skill specific to psychology, although it necessarily draws on the writer's previous education. Most authors agree that writing well in general, and writing reports well, specifically, is difficult. One reason is that English is not written in the same way that it is spoken. Competent speakers of English are not always competent writers. If psychologists simply write down exactly what they would say, the result is likely to be unintelligible. Therefore, translating ideas that may be expressed well in conversations with clients, parents, or colleagues into written English can be tricky.

Even when psychologists are competent at translating their ideas into written English, another problem remains. Report writing like any other skill must be practiced and the results critically examined for the skill to be mastered and maintained. Reports will not improve automatically with experience because little is learned when psychologists pull reports together hastily without taking time to reflect on their content and organization. They simply make the same mistakes repeatedly when report writing becomes automatic. For these reasons, psychologists often feel frustrated with the process of report writing and avoid it. If, in addition, they do not have a systematic method for putting their ideas into writing, or concrete guidelines for ways to improve their reports, the task of reporting becomes even more frustrating, possibly overwhelming.

This book addresses these problems in several ways. First, a theory-based outline of report writing problems is developed later in this chapter. The outline gives an organizing structure for understanding the problems implicit in report writing. It also helps to develop ways of addressing these problems. Second, chapter 2 presents a survey of research and expert opinion on psychological report writing. This survey shows what solutions to the problems highlighted in the outline already exist. You will probably see that most of the important issues in reporting have not been adequately researched. Guidance must often be drawn from a consensus of others' opinions about the language, organization, and content of reports.

Later in this book, several lines of research are synthesized into a concrete model for a specific method of writing sentences and paragraphs in reports. The model will help you decide the best way to organize your reports, depending on the setting in which you work. Differences between spoken and written English are discussed to clarify the best way of transforming your ideas about the assessment into clear and readable statements. The ideas that underlie the model will also help you to understand how to move from the raw data of the assessment to relevant statements about the person evaluated. How to organize the resulting sentences into paragraphs and the larger sections of the report is then discussed. Later chapters of the book review how to tailor your reports for use in specific contexts and across psychological specialties. Throughout, material for illustration and practice is provided. Appendixes A, B, and C provide still more material for learning the model and for diagnosing problems in your reports. Appendix D includes model reports that illustrate the principles discussed in the book.

This book will not make you a master of psychological report writing overnight, but the model and procedures described can help you to better define the task of report writing. Over time, use of the model and procedures should help you develop better report writing skills by encouraging you to: (1) reflect on how you write reports, (2) obtain feedback from your readers to help you understand potential problems, and (3) tailor the reports you write to the contexts in which they will be used. The model reports in Appendix D and the practice material in Appendixes A and B will help you master important points. But first, it is necessary to examine the theory of psychological report writing.

The Theory of Psychological Report Writing

Psychological report writing may not seem worthy of its own theory. Creating a theory of reporting may be taking the task too seriously, or making something that is obvious excessively formal. Research on reports, however, shows that consumers of reports are often dissatisfied with the product. Reports are often viewed as inadequate at best and as unintentionally malicious at worst. Research has shown that reports can affect how teachers view their competence in working with children who have learning or behavior problems. This suggests that reports can have negative effects, and thus psychologists should be careful not to cause harm when writing reports. A theory of reporting can help you to write reports that are more likely to be helpful to your clients.

Few researchers have approached the same questions in ways that allow comparisons of their findings. A theory of reporting allows co-ordination of investigative efforts. With a theory, then, research can identify important research questions, and results of current investigations can be related more easily to previous studies. Appropriate hypotheses for future studies can also be generated more readily.

The following outline of a theory for reporting is based on previous research and opinion on report writing. The ideas incorporated allow explicit consideration of critical variables. *Internal variables* are those inherent to the report itself, such as style, content, and format. *External variables* affect the report from outside, such as the setting in which or the purpose for which the report is written. The theory comprises a set of basic concepts and related ideas that detail the most important issues in report writing. The outline of these elements can, in turn, be used by interested researchers to generate testable hypotheses about reports. Major headings in the outline are comprehensive and can be used to coordinate results of other studies. What follows is an explanation of the theory's basic ideas, which will be used to organize the remainder of the book.

The first purpose of psychological reports is to communicate information about a client to an interested reader. The information should be communicated to the reader in a way that will change the reader's beliefs about or behavior toward the client. The words *first purpose* allow that the report may have other functions, such as providing a record of the assessment for future use. Still, the primary reason for writing a report is to persuade someone to accept or do something that the psychologist believes will benefit the client. An important implication of this idea is that reports must include statements that are credible (that is, belief-changing) or persuasive (behavior-changing) for the reader. This hypothesis has been tested several times, as shown in later discussions (Ownby, 1990a, 1990b; see chapter 2).

Reports can be analyzed according to their structure and content. The word *structure* is used broadly here to include the ways in which sentences, paragraphs, sections, and the entire report are put together. *Content* here refers only to general categories of material included in reports, such as test data, behavioral observations, or other information about a client's cognitive or emotional functioning. It may seem obvious that these types of analyses are possible, but this basic idea is essential to developing research strategies. Investigations of structure and content allow researchers to specify which structures and contents are most credible or persuasive.

How reports are organized can also be evaluated. Again, this may seem obvious, but this basic idea is a necessary preliminary to other studies. *Organized* here refers to the models, formats, and writing styles that can be used in writing reports. The implication is that research studies can be conducted to determine the best organizations for psychological reports.

How reports function in their contexts can be evaluated. The implication of this basic concept is that although relevant contextual variables are numerous and their interactions complex, the complexity can be reduced to a level that allows empirical investigation. This can be accomplished, for example, by establishing a few broad categories for contextual variables. These variables include the reasons underlying the initial request for assessment, the types of settings in which the report will be used, and the different professionals who will read the report (Ownby, 1986b; Ownby, Wallbrown, & D'Atri, 1984; Ownby, Wallbrown, D'Atri, & Armstrong, 1985).

Variables that are important for understanding report writing can be organized into a framework of categories. This idea simply justifies the structure of the entire outline. Three main categories of reporting variables are included: (1) structural, (2) organizational, and (3) contextual. These can be defined as follows:

1. *Structural*. These are internal variables that deal with how the basic elements of sentences, paragraphs, and the sections of the report are created. The expository process model, described in chapter 4, gives guidelines for dealing with structural issues by specifying how raw assessment data, theoretical constructs, conclusions, and recommendations should be organized. Only a few studies of structural variables in report writing are available (e.g., Ownby, 1984, 1990a, 1990b); these studies show that the expository process model is useful in deciding how to write sentences and paragraphs in reports.

The theory predicts that these variables should not change across different report organizations and settings. Research that addresses the best type of sentence structure in a report, for example, should be applicable whatever report organization is used, in whatever environment. Research supports this prediction (Ownby, 1984, 1990a, 1990b). This invariance is in marked contrast to the variance in the other two categories of factors, which interact with each other.

2. *Organizational*. These are also internal variables, but they define how sentences, paragraphs, and sections are organized in the report. They include model, format, and style. All involve the high-level organization of the report rather than the basic structure of sentences or paragraphs. They probably vary interactively with contextual variables. For example, the organization of a report written to help a teacher better understand one of his or her students will be different from that of a report written to a private physician who requested an evaluation of a patient to find out what part stress plays in an illness.

3. *Contextual*. These variables are external to the report and deal with how the report is affected by its context. These factors—referral agent, referral problem, and environment—vary across contexts and influence the basic organization of the report. The referral agent can vary by profession, level of training, and openness of agenda in making the referral. Referral problems vary by type of problem, and the referral environment varies in complexity. All of these variables should be considered in choosing a report's model, format, and style.

The effects of structural variables are constant across contexts. This implies that the best type of sentence, paragraph, or report section is the same whether the report is written by a clinical, counseling, or school psychologist for another psychologist, a physician, or an attorney. A corollary is the best way of dealing with structural variables can be defined through research. This corollary holds the promise that although reports must be tailored to their contexts, certain aspects of the report are invariant across situations. Every report does not have to be written as a completely new entity. You can learn to write good sentences and paragraphs and then use what you have learned consistently in all your reports. For example, if it were found that almost all reports should be written with a particular sentence structure and should include particular contents, your workload could be reduced considerably. This idea has received some support from research.

The effects of organizational variables change across contexts. In contrast to the structural issues discussed above, report factors such as model, format, and style should vary according to the referral agent, the referral problem, and the environment. A report written to another psychologist to be read only by him or her will be different from a report written to a public school teacher that might also be read by the school counselor or administrator. A corollary here is that reports are most likely to be effective when their organization is consistent with their context. One implication is that no one type of report will be best in all contexts. Another implication is that report writers must be flexible in their approach to reporting by explicitly assessing contextual variables and modifying the report's organization accordingly.

By organizing these basic ideas and their related concepts, we can construct a comprehensive outline of reporting variables (Figure 1.1). The outline allows for identification of testable research areas and for making predictions about the probable results of such research. The outline will be discussed further in chapter 9. The following example illustrates the usefulness of this outline, showing how it can organize testable hypotheses about report writing.

The theory of report writing states that the effects of structural variables in reports are constant across contexts or settings. The expository process model (see chapter 4) recommends specific ways of writing sentences and paragraphs in reports (Ownby & Wallbrown, 1986). The model for writing sentences states that certain content elements should be included in a particular order in each statement in a report. The model also predicts that the same structure should be effective in all contexts. Predictions about structural variables can be operationalized and the theory tested. Results support the proposition that structural variables are constant across contexts. Model-based statements have consistently been rated as more credible and persuasive across contexts.

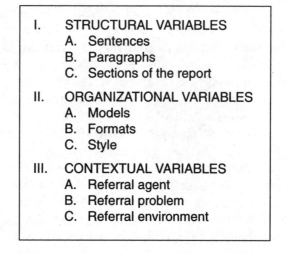

I.   STRUCTURAL VARIABLES
    A. Sentences
    B. Paragraphs
    C. Sections of the report

II.   ORGANIZATIONAL VARIABLES
    A. Models
    B. Formats
    C. Style

III. CONTEXTUAL VARIABLES
    A. Referral agent
    B. Referral problem
    C. Referral environment

Figure 1.1 Outline of Reporting Variables

The contextual variables include professional—psychologist, counselor, or social worker—and work settings—school, community mental health center, university, and psychiatric hospital—(Ownby, 1984, 1990a, 1990b).

The Practice of Psychological Report Writing

Kurt Lewin said, "There is nothing so practical as a good theory" (quoted by Marrow, 1969, p. viii). Lewin clearly understood the multiple roles a theory can play in influencing practice. There may be intrinsic value in developing a theory of reporting, but its most important function is to give writers guidance about how to write their reports. It is important to remember that reports have a significant impact on clients' welfare. The guidance function is particularly important because many questions about report writing have not been researched. A theory that is consistent with limited empirical findings can predict what may be true in other situations, even though they have not been researched. It is possible to act with a reasoned approach to a problem, even without extensive research.

An example may clarify how the theory can give guidance about report writing. Suppose you are asked to assess a child with a learning difficulty. What kind of report should you send to the child's teacher? To the child's physician? The theory tells you that the report's sentences and paragraphs should be written using the expository process model (chapter 4). Assessment of context (see chapter 6) allows you to make choices about appropriate organization. The report to the child's teacher, for example, might be domain-oriented (see chapter 5), depending on the relevance of ability domain to the child's problems and perhaps on your assessment of the teacher's interests. By contrast, the report to the physician might be hypothesis-oriented—perhaps the physician's primary interest is in knowing whether the child shows evidence of attention-deficit/hyperactivity disorder.

The format of the report should also be guided by your assessment of the report's context. The report to the child's teacher might be a brief or lengthy narrative, again depending on the teacher's interests. The report to the physician might be a brief narrative or even a letter. Both the domain- and hypothesis-oriented models can be integrated into brief formats. The style of your language will also be determined by your assessment of context. Most reports should be written in a professional style, especially when they will become a permanent record of your assessment. A letter to a physician, however, might be less formal.

This example illustrates how the outline of variables can give you a checklist for assessing how you write reports. The assessment guidelines included in Appendix B can also help you implement the theory in your report writing.

The rest of this book deals with the problems that arise in the practice of reporting psychological assessments. Keep the outline in mind so that you can relate it to the questions discussed in later sections in the book. Chapter 9 revisits the outline and reconsiders it in light of the evidence presented in the book.

2

RESEARCH ON REPORTS

Although writing reports is a critical part of many psychologists' jobs, little research exists on what makes reports effective. Thus, any review of what has been written about reports must focus more on expert opinion about reports than on empirical research. This chapter provides an overview of the literature on report writing. Although not exhaustive, this review includes many important references on report writing that show what others have viewed as problems with reports and how they have dealt with these problems. Additional references are provided in other chapters to illustrate important points.

Another aim of this chapter is to identify and clearly state the purposes of psychological reports so that better evaluation criteria can be formulated. When research findings are not available, opinions expressed by other authors are surveyed to develop a consensus on the problem. When no consensus can be reached, the best educated guess that can be made is offered.

Over several years, my colleagues and I have studied important aspects of report writing. We surveyed consumer satisfaction with reports written for special education teachers (Ownby, Wallbrown, & Brown, 1982) and proposed that using a questionnaire to obtain feedback about reports can help to improve them (Ownby & Wallbrown, 1983). We developed a classification system for referral problems in the schools that allows specification of the most useful report format (see chapter 5; Ownby et al., 1984; Ownby et al., 1985; Westman, Ownby, & Smith, 1987). We developed a model for writing reports based on a review of report writing research and a psycholinguistic model of discourse comprehension (Ownby, 1984, 1990a, 1990b; Ownby & Wallbrown, 1986).

We hope that this effort will supply needed information about reporting practices. Meanwhile, we can consider research findings and authorities' opinions and draw a consensus from them. Although organizing the following review according to the comprehensive outline presented in chapter 1 would be logical, it is not possible. Most of the studies reviewed do not focus on a single variable; most address several variables in the outline. This review is thus organized around broad topics such as the setting in which the research took place or the general issue on which the research focused.

Research in Clinical Settings

Research has shown that psychological reports in clinical settings are (a) sometimes considered useful by persons who receive the reports, such as psychiatrists and social workers; (b) frequently criticized by these professional groups on both content and stylistic grounds; and (c) may (or may not) make substantial contributions to client treatment planning.

In an early study, Garfield, Heine, and Leventhal (1954) examined views of psychological reports among three professional groups (psychologists, psychiatrists, and social workers) in a clinical setting. Psychiatrists criticized reports for including excessive speculation, for failing to include data from which inferences were drawn, and for vagueness and ambiguity in writing style. Psychologists also criticized the reports for failing to include the behavioral data from which inferences were drawn and for stylistic problems such as vagueness and the use of jargon. Social workers as a group were the least critical of reports.

Cuadra and Albaugh (1956) studied the relationship between what authors intended to write in reports and the message readers received. As they found at best a modest agreement between intended and received messages, Cuadra and Albaugh urged psychologists to be more careful to make their messages explicit in reports.

In a classic study of reports, Tallent and Reiss (1959a, 1959b, 1959c) compared three professional groups' opinions of report contents and found that psychologists, psychiatrists, and social workers showed

12

many common interests in the content of reports, as well as important differences. For example, while all three groups indicated that a general personality description and a discussion of dynamic defenses, interpersonal relations, and intellectual status were appropriate content, differences appeared on a few related issues. One area of divergence was on the issue of reporting IQ test results: "The psychiatrists and social workers appear to be more interested in having a statement of IQ or intelligence level than the psychologists are in reporting it" (1959a, pp. 218, 221). In addition, while 74% of the psychologists indicated that recommendations for treatment were appropriate content in reports, only 14% of the psychiatrists expressed this view. Apparently, the psychologists were more interested in giving an opinion than the psychiatrists were in receiving it.

Perhaps the most interesting result of Tallent and Reiss's study came from a sentence completion item included in their survey, the stem of which was, "The trouble with psychological reports is . . ." Tallent and Reiss obtained responses to this stem from a total of 712 psychologists, psychiatrists, and psychiatric social workers. The principal complaints of these professionals included "irresponsible interpretation" of data and "expressive deficiencies" (1959c, p. 446). Irresponsible interpretation in general referred to over- or underinterpretation of data or to statements that appeared to reflect the examiner's personality more than the client's. Expressive deficiencies referred to the use of jargon, wordiness, and ambiguity of content.

In a later study, Lacey and Ross (1964) examined the attitudes of three professional groups toward psychological reports in child guidance clinics. They found both similarities and differences between their results and those of Tallent and Reiss. Data were reported for a total of 150 psychologists, psychiatrists, and social workers in 10 child guidance clinics. One similarity between Lacey and Ross's results and Tallent and Reiss's was that workers in both settings believed that information about the client's appearance and behavior during assessment should be included in the report. An interesting difference between the two studies was that a larger percentage of professionals in the Lacey and Ross study felt that recommendations concerning client treatment should be included in the report. Another important difference between the two studies concerned the willingness of psychologists to include raw assessment data in the report (such as responses to projective test stimuli or observations of patient behavior during testing). Here, the psychologists in the child guidance setting were more willing to include these types of data in their reports. Lacey and Ross interpret this finding as showing that reports might be written differently depending on relationships between professional groups in varying settings. Finally, all three professional groups in this study reported much less dissatisfaction with expressive variables than those in Tallent and Reiss's study.

Hartlage, Freeman, Horine, and Walton (1968) used a different research strategy to determine the usefulness of statements frequently found in reports to psychiatrists who were making decisions with regard to clients. Hartlage et al. found a correlation of −.50 between a panel of psychiatrists' ratings of the usefulness of statements abstracted from a large number of reports and the frequency of these statements' appearance in reports. Hartlage et al. (1968) conclude that "it appears that this sample of psychological reports was evidently of little value in contributing toward any treatment decisions for the patients" (p. 483).

Moore, Boblitt, and Wildman (1968) surveyed a sample of psychiatrists in one institution, and a random sample of psychiatrists in the southeastern United States. They found that the majority of psychiatrists did not view psychological assessment as an essential part of client evaluation and that it "would not be used in any additional case planning even if changes were made in the structure of the report to make it more desirable" (p. 373). Among those psychiatrists who regularly used psychological evaluations as part of their treatment, however, Moore et al. (1968) found that they wanted the report to present a more detailed evaluation of client motivations, an outline of the client's problems, and suggestions about how to deal with them.

In another research study, Lacks, Horton, and Owen (1969) compared psychiatrists' satisfaction with a checklist report, a written outline report, and the standard narrative report. They found that many psychiatrists believe that standard psychological reports contain "too much irrelevant or needless information" and are often "too long, redundant, subjective, and over general" (p. 386). On the other hand, the information provided by the checklist alone was described as too limited. The written outline format received favorable ratings from psychiatrists, and Lacks et al. concluded that it might be used in settings in which there is pressure for prompt reporting of assessment data.

Affleck and Strider (1971) investigated the use of psychological reports in the development of client treatment plans in a psychiatric facility that provided both in- and outpatient services to children and adults. A total of 340 referral requests and reports and the reports' subsequent effects on treatment plans were investigated. In this study, persons who made referrals (usually psychiatric residents) were encouraged to indicate the types of information desired and to make specific referral requests. The authors concluded that the psychiatrists were provided with useful information, as "there is indication that 52% of the reports actually altered management in some direct way" (p. 179). These results contrasted with other negative evaluations of the usefulness of reports. It should be noted that the person who made the referral was asked to make specific information requests and to state the referral question clearly. This practice may have influenced the usefulness or relevance of the information obtained during the assessment by helping the psychologists give the psychiatrists the information they needed for client treatment.

More recently, several authors have commented on the function of evaluating clients as part of determining their eligibility for disability benefits and the role of reports in this process. Although these were not empirical studies of report writing, they are reviewed briefly here because of their relevance to report writing in clinical settings. Binder (1987) discussed the specific issue of the manner in which Wechsler Adult Intelligence Scale–Revised (WAIS-R) IQ and subtest scores should be reported. Binder noted that reporting age-corrected scores with older clients may be misleading if their performances are to be compared with those of younger persons. He argued for the use of non–age-corrected scores in such comparisons. This is a clinical setting example of the need to change reporting practices according to the purpose and context of the evaluation.

Kodimer (1988) discussed report writing in disability determinations more extensively. He suggested that one important reason for denial of disability benefits is inadequate reporting of assessment results. Kodimer reviewed Social Security Administration guidelines for disability determination and suggested ways of tailoring reports to communicate critical information most effectively. Kodimer proposed a number of specific issues that should be dealt with in these reports, such as the client's capacity for carrying out tasks of independent daily living, maintaining satisfactory interpersonal relations, and focusing attention in a sustained fashion. Reporting on these points, Kodimer asserted, would facilitate a review of the client's claim by Social Security. An inference to be drawn here is that, once again, it is important to tailor the report to its context.

Research in School Settings

The lack of research on the impact of psychological reports in school settings is especially disconcerting given the intense scrutiny that special education placement procedures have received, at least in part because of Public Law 94–142. This law mandates safeguards in the evaluation of and programming for children with special educational needs, areas in which school psychologists are often involved. Several authors have shown that special educators may be dissatisfied with aspects of school psychological services in general and with reports in particular (Gaddes, 1983; Keogh, 1972; Ownby, 1982; Ownby et al., 1982). Much research on school psychological reports has investigated teacher satisfaction with reports, although more recently the focus has been on determining how information from reports influences teacher attitudes and behaviors.

An early study by Mussman (1964) of teacher satisfaction with reports used 12 teachers as judges to evaluate a procedure in which they were given a brief handwritten report immediately after completion of the assessment. The traditional reports were forwarded to the teacher several weeks later in accordance with usual school system procedures. Evaluations of this process indicated that teachers preferred the immediate feedback report, but also valued the traditional report for its more extensive information and recommendations. Teachers stated that the reports could be improved by including observations of the child's behavior during assessment and by making the recommendations section of the report longer and more concrete.

Baker (1964) provided data about reports drawn from broader investigation of the perceptions of teachers, counselors, and administrators of psychological services in schools. In contrast to the negative findings of some studies, Baker asserted that "the claim that the reports of the school psychologists are commonly too technical, theoretical, or are written in a vague style, was not substantiated in this study. Teachers and counselors found information to be conveyed in a relatively coherent manner" (p. 39). An interesting and possibly significant finding of this study stems from Baker's comparison of the extent to which reports were useful to inexperienced teachers (less than four years of teaching) and experienced teachers (more than four years). Although "roughly half" (p. 39) of the inexperienced teachers responded that the report had added to their knowledge of the problem, only 28% of the experienced teachers made this response. This pattern shows that school psychologists may play a more important role in helping inexperienced teachers deal with student problems than in helping more experienced faculty.

Rucker (1967a) reported an investigation of teacher ratings of the usefulness of reports written by experienced psychologists versus less experienced psychologists and by psychologists with classroom teaching experience versus those without this experience. All comparisons among these groups were statistically nonsignificant, but the four elementary school teachers who served as judges contributed several valuable comments on the characteristics of useful reports. As a rule, the judges in Rucker's study stated that the more useful reports answered the referral questions clearly and "presented a well-rounded program consisting of a variety of specific recommendations to aid the teacher" (p. 105). Rucker also observed that the recommendations teachers judged most helpful were those that showed the writer understood how the recommendations might be implemented in the classroom.

In a second study, Rucker (1976b) investigated the degree to which commonly used terms in psychological reports represent meaningful communication rather than jargon to teachers, by comparing agreement between groups of psychologists and elementary school teachers on the meanings of such terms. Rucker's findings showed that even psychologists disagreed among themselves on the definitions of some terms and that there were even greater disagreements between psychologists and teachers. Rucker concluded that psychologists should use fewer technical terms and write reports in language that is likely to be clear to the report's intended recipient.

Brandt and Giebink (1968) studied ways in which the concreteness of recommendations and the congruence of interpretations of child behavior with teacher attitudes affect teacher preferences for reports. They found that teachers preferred reports whose interpretations indicated an accepting attitude toward the child regardless of whether such an attitude was congruent with their own. Brandt and Giebink concluded that their results support others' emphases on the need for providing specific recommendations in reports.

A study by Shively and Smith (1969) examined the extent to which teachers, counselors, and undergraduate teacher-education students understood terms frequently used in reports. Their findings indicated that although counselors understood more of the technical terms drawn from a sample of reports than did the other two groups, only 54% of the technical terms were understood overall.

Noting "a surprising lack of published material which documents the effectiveness of the practice of preparing diagnostic reports," Waugh (1970, p. 631) reported an investigation of the issue. Graduate students at a university learning-disabilities clinic prepared reports after they had worked with children for 25 hours over an 8-week period. The reports were given to each child's classroom teacher, and 2 weeks later a questionnaire was sent to the teachers. Waugh found that 61% of the reports were rated as useful in planning for the child, but only 23 questionnaires were returned. Waugh concluded that "emphasis on educational deficits does improve the impact of the psycho-diagnostic reports" (p. 632). It must be noted, however, that Waugh drew this conclusion from a comparison of her results with those of the study by Baker (discussed above). Waugh's conclusion is questionable in light of the small number of questionnaires returned in her sample, the fact that the questions asked of the respondents in the two studies were not the same, and the possible differences between the two groups of teachers.

In a dissertation study, Sudduth (1976) investigated the effects of three methods of reporting assessment data to teachers. After an assessment was completed, teachers received one of four combinations of report and consultation: (a) written report only; (b) face-to-face consultation only; (c) report and consultation; or (d) no report or consultation. The report and consultation group showed significant increases in teacher–psychologist agreement about the nature of the problem, but no other significant treatment effects were observed. This finding supports the idea that the report, in conjunction with consultation, is an important part of providing school psychological services.

Also in a dissertation study, Littlejohn (1977) compared preferences for three report formats among school psychologists, elementary teachers, elementary principals, and educators of school psychologists. Formats studied were (a) traditional narrative; (b) brief checklist; and (c) brief narrative with emphasis on recommendations. A central finding was that all groups showed the strongest preference for the traditional narrative format. Littlejohn also asked participants to rank the sections of the report in order of importance. All groups ranked the recommendations section as most useful.

Isett and Roszkowski (1979) studied the value of various sections of the report for workers in a short-term residential facility for developmentally disabled persons. They found that the reports' users believed that recommendations and information about the clients' social competence were most valuable and that projective test data and IQ test results were least valuable in their work with these clients.

Bagnato (1980) examined differences between two styles of writing diagnostic reports. A group of 48 teachers in early childhood handicapped education programs received training in developing curricular objectives from assessment data. They were then asked to develop educational programs for students either from traditional psychological reports or from "translated" reports whose recommendations were keyed to specific developmental curriculum goals. Bagnato found that the "translated" reports were superior to the traditional reports in helping teachers to develop educational programs. Bagnato made the following recommendations about reports: (a) they should be organized by ability domain rather than by test; (b) they should describe strengths and weaknesses in behavioral terms; (c) they should emphasize process variables, such as learning strategies; (d) they should link assessment tasks closely to curricular goals in order to facilitate educational plan development; and (e) they should provide teachers with recommendations for behavioral management techniques.

In a study of how teachers view reports from clinical psychologists, Berry (1975) found that even though about 30% believed that there was too much psychological terminology in reports and that the reports were neither clear nor lucid, 65% were generally satisfied with the reports they had received. Also of interest are Berry's findings that 86% of the teachers wanted the report to help them in making decisions about the child and that 61% rated the specific recommendations section as the most useful part of the report in working with the child. The return rate of Berry's questionnaire, however, was only 46%.

Finally, Ownby et al. (1982) investigated special education teachers' perceptions of reports. They found that important components of each section of the report (for example, observations of a child's behavior in the classroom or a discussion of his or her social-emotional status) were included with varying frequency in reports received by the teachers. This finding suggests that important report elements were sometimes omitted. They also found that reports received by these teachers often did not include a statement of the test results' validity, even though numerous authorities recommended that such a statement be included. Another finding was that while behavioral observations were often included in reports, the behaviors observed were rarely linked to antecedent behaviors. This suggests that although psychologists may have believed that the child's behavior was important, they did not systematically assess it in order to design strategies for changing it.

In the 1980s, studies generally began to focus more closely on specific issues about reporting that are amenable to empirical investigation. This trend represented a transition from studies that merely documented consumers' dissatisfaction with reports to attempts to study reporting variables and their effects on the process of communication with readers. For example, Witt, Moe, Gutkin, and Andrews (1984) studied the effects of different types of jargon on teachers' acceptance of potential classroom interventions for behavior problems. They developed essentially identical interventions for both mild and severe behavior problems and couched them in either behavioristic, humanistic, or pragmatic (e.g., logical consequences) terms. They found that interventions phrased pragmatically (e.g., staying in from recess for not completing work) were rated as more acceptable than the same interventions phrased in other terms.

Weddig (1984) reviewed 50 psychological reports and determined their reading levels. She then drew one report from the sample that had a median reading difficulty and made it more readable by changing vocabulary, replacing professional terminology with behavioral descriptions, and removing irrelevant information. Parents were then asked to read either the original or the modified report and were tested for their comprehension of the content. Weddig concluded that her modifications made the report more understandable for the parents and recommended that psychologists use readability measures in evaluating their reports. She also made the specific recommendations that psychologists should write reports at a lower level of reading difficulty, should replace professional terms with descriptions of behaviors, and should remove content not related to the placement decision.

Wiener, in a series of studies (1985, 1987; Wiener & Kohler, 1986), has worked to define variables related to consumers' satisfaction with and comprehension of psychological reports. Consistent with results of other studies, Wiener found that teachers better understood reports that organized information according to ability areas, described strengths and weaknesses in behavioral terms rather than jargon, and clearly explained recommendations (Wiener, 1985). In this study, Wiener also found that teachers preferred reports that explicitly responded to the referral questions. In other studies, Wiener found similar results with groups of parents and with groups of other educators (Wiener, 1985; Wiener & Kohler, 1986). This series of studies is particularly important because they addressed not only consumers' preferences, but also consumers' understanding of the information conveyed by the report. These studies confirmed the relationship between consumer preference and consumer ability to acquire desired information.

Hagborg (1993) studied how well parents understood the results of psychological assessments, including the psychological report. Hagborg showed good agreement between parents and the psychologist on much of the information found during the assessment. It should be emphasized that Hagborg studied reports in combination with a post-assessment conference. Although limited by the small number of children evaluated and the use of only one psychologist's work, this study showed that the combination of report and oral presentation effectively communicates assessment information to consumers.

Finally, Tanner (1993, 1994) showed how writing a report can be automated to save time. Tanner noted the inherent problem of working in a teaching hospital where assessment results must be provided rapidly but where assessments may be done by trainees who are not able to produce reports quickly. He developed a computer program that uses templates for many routine parts of the report, for example, identifying information, certain parts of the background information, and reporting specific test data. Narrative sections of the report are written by the psychologist or trainee and automatically inserted in the appropriate place in the report.

This type of report format has also been developed for other assessments (see almost any catalog of psychological testing materials). The advantages of this approach are clear: speed, standardization, and flexibility in reporting assessments. On-screen checklists ensure that important points (for example, key historical variables) are at least considered while writing the report. Disadvantages of this approach included the temptation to standardize excessively leading to stereotyped reports that do not provide a clear picture of the person assessed.

Biasing Information in Reports

An important area of recent research on report writing deals with the effects of biasing information in reports on teachers' perceptions of and behaviors toward children. Usually, these studies bear most directly on school psychological reports, but they are relevant to report writing in other specialties as well. Interest in this area may have been sparked by Rosenthal and Jacobson's (1968) pioneering work, which showed that teacher expectations based on information about children's abilities may have an effect on children's eventual classroom success. While these studies bypassed the as yet unresolved issue of whether reports do, in fact, affect teachers' behaviors, the significant effects of biasing information on teachers' beliefs suggested that reports are influential in attitude change. However, studies that have examined this issue have not shown consistently that reports have a significant impact on teachers' attitudes or behaviors.

Robinson (1974) studied the effects of two methods of psychological service delivery on children's group achievement test performance. This research was somewhat artificial in that the children involved were not referred for problems, but were chosen from all children in a school system's third-grade class. The 39 children selected were administered a standard battery of tests. In one treatment condition, teachers received a test report written in jargon and did not have a conference with the psychologist, while in a second condition, test results were reported in a conference and in a clearly written report that included detailed recommendations. Even with such extreme differences in service delivery, children's group achievement test scores did not vary significantly between conditions after 3 months. Further, teachers' ratings of the children's improvement in scholastic abilities did not vary either.

In an investigation suggesting that reports may influence teachers' perceptions of students, Mertens (1976) studied the effects of biased reports on teachers' ratings of student essays. A group of 94 teachers in training were given biased reports about a hypothetical child. They were then asked to rate an essay by the child and fill out a report card on the child according to their expectations for the child's achievement at the end of the school year. Results showed that biasing information in reports can influence teacher perceptions of student performance (ratings of the essay) and their expectations for student success (estimated end-of-year grades).

Schwartz (1977) showed that certain types of information in reports may differentially influence teachers' perceptions of children. Schwartz provided either information about what to do with a child who was exhibiting problems ("Type I") or explanatory information about the child's behavior ("Type II"). This study showed that Type I information positively changed teachers' perceptions of the child's ability to improve, of the child's potential to be disruptive, and of the teachers' ability to deal with the child's difficulties in the classroom. Type II information positively changed teachers' perceptions of the child's degree of exceptionality and their emotional reactions to the child.

Schwartz and Wilkinson (1987) studied the effects of diagnostic labels provided in mocked-up school folders on teachers' reactions to report contents. They found that diagnostic labels affected how teachers interpreted data in reports (even when the data contradicted the proposed diagnostic label) and concluded that "teachers' perceptions of various types of exceptional children are differentially affected by the unique combinations of prior expectation, report data and interpretation, and the specific kinds of academic and social/emotional behavior under consideration" (p. 134).

These studies showed that information provided in psychological reports has the potential to affect teachers' perceptions of and expectations for students. The nature of these effects is clearly complex—Schwartz's study, for example, showed that the type of information may interact with the type of attitude or belief change obtained. The relations between information, expectations, and teacher behavior are still more complex, as suggested by Robinson's failure to find a significant impact of report information on children's academic achievement test scores. Mertens's results, however, are consistent with the idea that the favorability of information provided to teachers may influence their expectations for student performance.

As a group, these studies showed that reports may have an important impact on teacher perceptions and expectations, but they failed to draw a clear conclusion about the nature of this impact and its ultimate meaning for teacher behavior. In all specialties, it is probably prudent to include information in the report about the client's strengths and weaknesses, to explain why the client functions as he or she does, and to provide specific recommendations (when desired by the referring agent) about how to work with the client.

Barnum Effect

An important area of research in test interpretation and reporting concerns the Barnum effect. This effect arises from the observation that personality interpretations that are sufficiently vague are true of most persons (Dana & Fouke, 1979; Forer, 1949; O'Dell, 1972; M. Smith, 1986; Sundberg, 1955). Dickson and Kelly provided examples of several categories of Barnum statements. Some are vague, such as, "you enjoy a certain amount of change and variety in life"; some are *double-headed*, such as "you are generally cheerful and optimistic but get depressed at times"; some describe *modal characteristics of the subject's group*, such as "you find that study is not always easy"; and some are frankly positive, such as "you are forceful and well-liked by others" (1985, p 367).

Although few, if any, studies have demonstrated that Barnum statements are a significant problem in reports that are actually used in practice, it is apparent that such statements could easily be incorporated into reports and uncritically accepted by readers. The result would be reports that are speciously acceptable to readers and give writers a false sense of having communicated something important about the client. The problem of the Barnum effect is discussed more fully later in this chapter and in chapter 3.

Improving Reports

Several authors have discussed ways of improving reports. Hartlage and Merck (1971), for example, asked supervisors in a rehabilitation facility to rank 31 frequently occurring statements drawn from reports according to their usefulness in helping them plan for clients. Information about the usefulness of various statements to supervisors was then made available to the psychologists whose reports were used in creating the list of frequently occurring statements. Hartlage and Merck then chose 20 reports each from the 4-month periods prior and subsequent to the feedback and asked supervisors to rate them. Hartlage and Merck found a "clear and consistent" (p. 460) superiority of new versus old reports and suggested that the change was due not to a shift in the types of data presented in the reports, but to the more valuable way in which data were presented to the supervisors. Hartlage and Merck stated that "reports can be made more relevant to their prospective users merely by having the psychologists familiarize themselves with the uses to which their reports are to be applied" (p. 460). They conclude that psychologists ought "to evaluate their own reports in terms of what these reports contribute to the operation of their unique settings rather than to continue to grind out reports with good theoretical consistency but little decisional value" (p. 460).

Taking into account these findings, as well as other report research, Ownby and Wallbrown (1983) argued for the importance of obtaining specific feedback about reports as a way of improving them. They presented a brief evaluative questionnaire to accompany each report as a way of learning whether a report answered the referral question, provided useful information and recommendations, and contained any terms that were difficult for its recipient to understand. In light of the substantial effect that feedback can have on a report's effectiveness, such a procedure may provide report writers with critically important information with which to improve their reporting practices. Subsequently, this approach was also suggested by Sattler (1988).

Weddig (1984), in a study discussed more extensively above, argued for the use of readability formulae in making reports more understandable. Pryzwansky and Hanania (1986) applied research on experts' problem-solving behavior (e.g., Sloves, Docherty, & Schneider, 1979) to the organization of psychological reports. They suggested that consumers might prefer reports organized according to these principles, which require a sequence of activities in problem solving that move from abstract statement of the problem to particular solutions. In contrast to the expected preference, however, Pryzwansky and Hanania (1986) found a strong preference for the traditional report organization. They concluded that "attempts to improve the quality of psychological reports by changing their organization may be analogous to fixing something that is not broken" (p. 139).

Computers and the Report

Computers have played an increasingly important role in psychological assessment. Even a quick scan of test publishers' catalogs shows that many tests can now be scored and interpreted by computer; many of these computer programs offer welcome relief from tedious statistical calculations and provide convenient tabulations of numerical data for measures ranging from the Wechsler Intelligence Scales to the Rorschach and the Minnesota Multiphasic Personality Inventory. Many of these programs result in narrative interpretations of assessment data that may be included in the final assessment report.

Several authors have investigated the possibility that readers of reports may view computer-generated reports more favorably than traditional reports. Crimando and Bordieri (1991) studied rehabilitation counseling students' perceptions of reports when they believed the reports were prepared by an experienced assessor or by a computer program. They also studied the relationship of report quality to students' ratings by providing two reports—the "good" report was prepared according to standard guidelines for good practice, while the "poor" report included unfounded generalizations, unexplained abbreviations, and grammatical errors. In an analysis of variance of ratings of the reports on variables including utility, specificity, and length, Crimando and Bordieri found a consistent effect for quality of report. They also found an interaction of quality by perceived origin of the report, with poor reports perceived as more useful when participants believed they had been prepared by computer. This study provided some evidence for the idea that a positive halo effect may occur for computer-generated reports.

By contrast, Andrews and Gutkin (1991) studied the effect of computer versus human authorship on readers' perceptions of a school psychological report. They asked 60 school personnel (mostly elementary school teachers, but also small groups of specialists such as special education teachers or counselors) to rate the same two-page report. Participants were randomly assigned to one of two conditions in which they were told that either a computer or a doctoral-level school psychologist had written the report. Andrews and Gutkin found no differences in ratings of overall quality, credibility, quality of diagnostic interpretations, or level of confidence in the judgments made in the report. They suggested that perhaps this was because readers paid more attention to the report's content (which was the same in both conditions) than to the more peripheral issue of report authorship.

Rubenzer (1992) compared ratings of a traditional psychological report with the computerized report generated for the Millon Adolescent Personality Inventory (Millon, Green, & Meagher, 1982). Reports focused on adolescent psychiatric inpatients in a medical hospital. Twenty-one typical consumers of reports (nurses, therapists, and other mental health workers) were asked to rate the reports, but not all reports were rated by all raters. An interesting aspect of this study was inclusion of accuracy ratings; clinicians who had worked with the patients reported on were asked to rate the accuracy of each report format. Rubenzer found that the traditional report was not more accurate than the computerized report, and was in fact rated as having less specificity and poorer quality writing. Therapists, however, preferred the traditional format. The average accuracy rating for all reports fell between "adequate" and "good" (p. 825). These findings were discussed by Rubenzer considering that computerized reports are much less expensive than the more complete psychological assessment and can be obtained much more quickly.

These three studies varied in quality of design and execution, and they examined different types of reports in different settings. Results suggested that computerized reports may be at least as useful to readers as traditional reports, and that a positive halo effect may result when a report is generated by a computer. Overall, though, results of these studies confirmed the basic observations made by others that the quality of the report is more important than its author, and reports that contain unfounded generalizations, jargon, unidentified abbreviations, and grammar errors are viewed more negatively than reports that avoid these errors. Thus it is apparent that authors should strive to avoid common pitfalls and to write well in creating their reports.

Purposes of Psychological Reports

Many authors have reviewed the purposes of psychological reports. This issue is critical because explicitly defining the reasons for writing reports is necessary in order to evaluate the extent to which reports accomplish their goals. A definition of purpose can also help writers decide how to write reports. What most authorities suggest about reports' purposes, however, appears to be based on clinical experience, theoretical orientation, or personal preference rather than on empirical research. Research on the purposes of reports might clarify, for example, the functions that reports serve in particular contexts. It is conceivable that one type of report might be useful in recording the results of an assessment for future use, another type might be useful in communicating technical data to other professionals, and yet another type might be most effective in changing readers' beliefs and behaviors. Research on the appropriate goals of report writing across contexts is not available, which makes it difficult to define these questions further. For example, in one of the few studies of content variables in reports, Sinclair and Alexson (1986) found that information about academic achievement was critical in psychoeducational reports, while information about medical background was unrelated to placement. This result showed that defining the purpose of reports is an important prerequisite to determining their effectiveness.

As in other areas, the purpose of this review must be limited to defining a consensus among authorities. Central issues on which a consensus emerged are: (a) the report should be written with the needs of the referring person in mind; (b) reports should provide information that is relevant to the reader's work with the client, but that may not have been requested; (c) reports should communicate in a way that is appropriate to the report's intended recipient; and (d) reports should affect the way the reader works with the client.

Most authorities agreed on the importance of considering the questions that the report is to answer. Sundberg and Tyler (1962), for example, stated that "as he [or she] organizes the material into a report, the foremost guide the clinician has in mind is: What are the questions this report is to answer—the purpose of this assessment work?" (p.228). They also noted that the written report may include not only answers to questions posed in the original referral, but also new information discovered in the assessment process that may be useful to the report's recipients. Huber (1961) echoed this point of view, stating that "the function of a report is to answer questions (p. 1), as did Klopfer (1960), who suggested that the report should contain practical information that would help those who were working with the client to determine appropriate courses of action.

Another point on which experts agreed is the importance of considering the context in which the report is to serve. Here, the purpose of the report is implicitly to communicate assessment information in a way that is easily comprehensible to the referring person. Harrower (1965), for example, suggested that the report writer should be thoroughly familiar with the context into which the report is sent. Appelbaum (1970) went even further in suggesting that the problem with psychological reports lies not so much with the reports themselves, but with writers' failure to recognize their multiple roles in providing assessment information. Appelbaum argued that "the test report is part of a complex and dynamic social system" (p. 350) and that psychologists' roles in this system include those of politician, diplomat, salesman, and artist, depending on the situations in which test data (whose purpose is to affect how others deal with clients) are communicated. Appelbaum's position, therefore, was that the purpose of reports is to communicate assessment information in a fashion appropriate to the intended reader so that the way the reader works with the client is affected. With respect to stylistic issues, Appelbaum recommended that the writer of the report strike a balance between the use of raw data and abstract statements, make appropriate use of technical language, and provide reasonable estimates of the confidence with which conclusions are drawn. He also suggested that the writer should try to make the report interesting to the reader.

Palmer's (1970) viewpoint on reports is illustrated by this statement: "It should be written to and for the referrant. It should reply clearly and succinctly to the referrant's questions" (p. 336). Palmer recognized that the assessment may also produce data that are relevant to the treatment of the client, but are not directly related to referral questions, and recommended that these data be included. Palmer did not explicitly comment on whether reports should attempt to affect work with clients, although it seems likely from the tone of the text that he would endorse this view.

In the first edition of his text on assessment of children, Sattler (1974) specified three purposes of report writing: "To answer the referral question, to convey in as much depth as possible a meaningful description of the examinee, and to provide useful recommendations" (1974, p. 368). Sattler's view of the assessment procedure is thus somewhat broader than that of other authorities in that he makes explicit the idea that providing a description of the person assessed is itself also a legitimate goal of the report. In a more recent edition of this work, Sattler (1982, p. 510) summarized his position again: "Psychological reports

29

(a) provide a record of the child's performance; (b) communicate findings; (c) help in providing remediation suggestions; and (d) facilitate placement decisions." Thus, Sattler viewed the psychological report as serving several purposes: recording, describing, and affecting work with clients.

In his comprehensive text on report writing, Tallent (1976) offered the following definition of a report, in it addressing the purpose of reports: "The psychological report may be defined as a document written as a means of understanding certain features about a person and his circumstances in order to make decisions about, for, or with him, and to intervene positively in his life" (p. 10). Thus, both Sattler and Tallent suggested that reports should serve multiple functions, and while Sattler proposed a somewhat wider range, Tallent emphasized that the report should help to change something in the client's life. Shea (1985) argued that "the purpose of the report is to communicate *effectively* with the reader" (1985, pp. 7–8; emphasis in the original). Shea went on to suggest that the report should function as an independent document that communicates "who the client is, why the assessment was performed, what was found, and what recommendations were proposed" (p. 8).

In a similar vein, Schwartz (1987) argued that the "primary purpose of psychological reports is to communicate test findings clearly" (p. 289). He went on to say that reports should answer referral questions and lead to effective interventions on behalf of the client. Gregory (1987) also emphasized the importance of answering referral questions. Blau (1991) noted that the result of a child psychological assessment should be a "report that is useful in advancing the best interests of the child" (p. 197). He suggested that the main goal of the report is to create a "realistic picture of the child" (p. 197). Subordinate but still important goals of the report were to convey information so that others understand the child, and "to offer realistic opportunities to intervene in a positive manner" (p. 197). These authors thus also supported the ideas that reports should explicitly target referral questions and should make recommendations that will affect others' work with clients.

A review of these authorities' opinions indicates substantial consensus on certain aspects of reports' purposes. Nearly all authorities stated, logically enough, that the report should respond directly to the referral agent's questions. Nearly all also stated that the report should provide data in a way that is comprehensible to the intended reader. Several authorities suggested that the report should provide a description of the client and a record of the psychologist's assessment activities. Virtually all the experts agreed, either explicitly or implicitly, that the report should affect the way the recipient works with the client.

From these observations it is possible to offer a tentative statement on the purposes of psychological reports. The purposes of such reports are:

1. to answer referral questions as explicitly as possible, depending on how well defined the questions are;
2. to provide the referring agent with additional information when it is relevant to his or her work with the client and when it is appropriate for the use to which the report will be put (this includes providing a general description of the client);
3. to make a record of the assessment activities for future use; and
4. to recommend a specific course of action for the recipient of the report to follow in his or her work with the client.

Clearly, the overriding purpose of the psychological report should be to influence the way in which the report's reader deals with the client. Whether the report is answering questions, describing a client, or recording assessment data, it should provide statements that alter the reader's beliefs about and behaviors toward the client. Thus, the report should provide statements that are *credible* (to change beliefs) and *persuasive* (to change behaviors). This is the definition of the purpose of reports used throughout the remainder of this book.

Literature on Reporting: Summary

The varied nature of the research on report writing reviewed here shows that few of the important issues about reporting have been researched adequately. As a result, it is not always possible to arrive at research-based decisions about how to write reports. Inferences can, however, be drawn from the review to provide tentative guidance about structural, content, organizational, and contextual variables. Thus, you can use research data and the consensus drawn from expert opinion to determine the most effective strategies for writing your reports. These inferences are sketched briefly in the remainder of this chapter; subsequent chapters provide more complete discussions of how to implement the guidelines in your day-to-day practice. Issues discussed in the rest of this book include how to write sentences, paragraphs, and sections in the report; what material reports should contain; how reports should be organized; and how reports should be tailored to their contexts.

Writing

A review of problems in report writing suggests that writers do not always appreciate the importance of basic composition skills. Although a course in basic writing skills is beyond the scope of this book, a discussion of the relationship of spoken English to written English may help you appreciate the importance of approaching writing as a special form of communication. Chapter 4 presents a discussion of this relationship and introduces a psycholinguistic model for writing reports.

Structural Variables

One of the few things that appears certain from a review of the research on reporting is that reports often contain terms whose meanings are unclear to the recipients. Nearly every author who has written about reports cautions writers not to use jargon. This suggestion appears especially important in light of findings such as Rucker's (1967b), which showed that groups of typical report readers, and even psychologists themselves, disagree on the meanings of widely used terms. Virtually every writer who has commented on reports has argued against the use of technical vocabulary in reports, and many have suggested substitution of behavioral descriptions. The importance of this issue is also highlighted by evidence that even the type of jargon used can influence the acceptability of recommended interventions (Witt et al., 1984). It is clear that psychological terms should be used cautiously in reports, both because such terms may be confusing to the reader and because they may affect his or her willingness to implement recommendations contained in the report.

A related problem stems from disagreement over the extent to which data such as behavior during testing should be included in the report. Research on readers' preferences shows that they want the writer to include some of the raw data on which reports are based, but it is not clear how the writer is to select appropriate data and how he or she is to relate these data to conclusions and recommendations. The central task for the writer is to turn the raw data of the assessment into meaningful conclusions and recommendations. At some point in writing the report, he or she must decide how to move from basic data to more general statements about client function. It is at this point that many psychologists are likely to use terms that are not meaningful to the report's readers. The problem, then, may not be so much the terms themselves as their relationship to other material in the report. These problems are addressed in chapter 4 on the expository process model.

Content Variables

Issues in this area range from determining the extent to which the report is to provide a broad picture of the client's functioning versus answering only specific questions to whether test scores should be included in the report. Studies that show the effects of biasing information suggest the importance of providing information about the client's strengths as well as the client's weaknesses. If information in the report depicts a client with many problems and few resources for coping, the report reader may become pessimistic about the client's chances for improvement. Schwartz's (1977) finding that information about how to deal with a child may enhance teachers' belief in their ability to cope with the difficulties the child presents underscored the need for a specific and detailed recommendations section in most reports. It may also be apparent that content issues cannot be separated arbitrarily from structural issues: the determination of how much and what sort of data to include in the report is at once an issue of both style and content. Content issues are discussed further in chapter 7.

Organizational Variables

Defining the differences between organization and content is not easy either. Many authorities (e.g., Hollis & Donn, 1979; Klopfer, 1960; Tallent, 1976) have suggested formats for reports, and there is considerable agreement among authorities on the basic elements of these formats. It is also possible to deduce a report format based on the report's purpose. Chapter 7 on report organization addresses these concerns and shows how reports can be tailored to function within various contexts and for various purposes.

Purposes of the Report

Even in the basic area of deciding precisely what the report should do there is no obvious consensus. Most authors do, however, agree that the report should serve at least four purposes: (a) describing the client assessed and the client's problem; (b) recording the results of the evaluation for future use; (c) communicating the results of the assessment to interested persons; and (d) recommending an appropriate course of action. Several authors (Appelbaum, 1970; Tallent, 1976, 1980) argued that the report should serve what may be conveniently described as an influencing function in working to persuade the reader to alter his or her beliefs about the client and to undertake a particular course of action with respect to the client. These opinions allow the consensus that reports should affect the reader's beliefs and behaviors by providing statements that are credible and persuasive.

Referral Problem

A critical problem in writing the report is determining precisely what the referral question is and how to answer it as clearly as possible in a way suitable to the referring agent. Affleck and Strider (1971) showed that a clear specification of the referral problem and an equally specific attempt to address it may make the report more useful in planning for working with the client. Ways of addressing this issue are discussed in chapter 6.

Referral Context

Both authorities and researchers strongly recommend that the writer consider the context of the report while writing it. This entails understanding the referral agent, the client's environment, and the broader context in which interventions are to be made. These issues are discussed in chapter 6.

3
THE IMPLICIT CONTRACT BETWEEN READER AND WRITER

A central difficulty for many writers is understanding the complex relationship between spoken and written English. A review of problems with psychological reports shows that writers sometimes try to write without considering this complex relationship, with predictably poor results. Herbert Clark (Clark, 1985; Clark & Clark, 1977; Clark & Haviland, 1977; Wilkes-Gibbs & Clark, 1992) developed a model for understanding interactions between speakers and listeners that can be applied to the implicit interactions between writers and readers. This chapter presents a few basic ideas about discourse comprehension— ways that people understand oral language. These ideas are then applied to report writing to show how writers can create sentences and paragraphs that readers will readily understand. Later in this book, other report writing problems are discussed and the psycholinguistic framework developed in this chapter is expanded into a model that suggests solutions to these problems.

Before addressing the problems specific to report writing, it is useful to detail how some psycholinguistic ideas about discourse comprehension can be applied to written English. Later in this chapter, examples are provided so that you can practice using these ideas in reporting test data. First, you need to understand an elementary but critical distinction: how written English differs from spoken English.

Written and Spoken English

Written English bears a deceptively simple relationship to the spoken language. The vocabulary and syntax of written English (the way words are organized into sentences) may seem familiar, but when you write down what you might say to someone else, it usually doesn't read sensibly and may be misleading or impossible to understand. Why is this so? Imagine the following situation. A young psychologist arrives at a group office on Monday morning looking forward to having a cup of coffee and a donut. She expects them to be there, based on her past experience that someone at the office will have made coffee by the time she arrives and that another person will have purchased donuts. When she actually arrives, however, she sees a colleague taking the last donut from the box. The secretary, sympathetic to the psychologist's plight, responds to her questioning look with "He took the last one." In this situation, it is immediately clear to the psychologist what the secretary means. "He" refers to the colleague, "took" to the activity of removing the donut from the box, and "last one" to the only remaining donut.

Now imagine that the psychologist arrives at her office on the same morning, but before going to look for coffee and donuts, she finds a note on her desk. The thoughtful secretary has left a message: "He took the last one." It should be immediately apparent that the psychologist will have to ask the secretary for clarification of the message.

This example shows that speakers rely on many sources of information in addition to the words used in oral communication. As we speak, we consciously and unconsciously take in listeners' facial expressions and postures. In addition, we share context. In the example above, the context of the communication determined to a great extent the meaning of the message. When communication is in written form, as in psychological reports, these aids are not present; much more of the communication burden falls on the meaning of the words themselves and on their organization. The writer must carefully assess the extent to which the reader will comprehend the context of the communication. For example, discussion of psychological test data in a report takes place in contexts that are quite different when reader and writer are both psychologists than when one is a lay person. These facts require the writer to develop expertise in using more restricted tools for communicating the complex ideas contained in psychological reports.

The Given-New Contract

Clark (Clark, 1985; Clark & Clark, 1977; Clark & Haviland, 1977) suggests that during a conversation an implicit contract exists between speaker and listener. This is part of the general process known as *coordination*, by which speakers and listeners cooperate in the communication process so that they are mutually intelligible (Clark, 1985). Clark calls this the *given-new contract*, emphasizing the essential requirement that two persons engaging in effective communication must agree on a basic idea (the *given*) before something can be said about it (the *new*). Clark and Clark (1977) explain:

> The speaker agrees (a) to use given information to refer to information she thinks the listener can uniquely identify from what he already knows and (b) to use new information to refer to information she believes to be true but is not already known to the listener. (p. 92)

In the example above, the secretary uses the word "He" in a context in which it clearly refers to the colleague taking the donut; "He" is the given element in the sentence. The new element is "took the last one."

A similar contract exists between reader and writer. Evidence on reading comprehension shows that prior knowledge influences how much a reader understands, a finding that supports the extension of the given-new contract concept to written prose (e.g., Entin & Klare, 1985). In order for the reader to feel that the writer has communicated effectively (indeed, to understand the writer at all), this contract cannot be violated. What circumstances, then, can result in a violation, and how can they be avoided?

In the context of the psychological report, the given-new contract can be violated at three points in the sequence: (1) the *given* may not, in fact, be shared information; (2) the link between *given* and *new* may not be logical; and (3) the new information may not be explained clearly or may not be unique new information about the given.

The first type of violation occurs when the given element is not a *shared referent*. Shared referents are whatever the psychologist can reasonably assume that he or she has in common with the reader. A concrete description of the client's behavior, such as "His voice trembled and was quite low as he spoke," provides an image with which the reader is probably familiar, and the psychologist can assume it constitutes a shared referent. On the other hand, a statement such as "The primed 2-7 profile code suggests the presence of considerable anxiety and depression" may be meaningless to readers not trained in MMPI interpretation, to whom the phrase "primed 2-7 code" will be jargon. Thus, one way in which the given-new contract can be violated in psychological reports is by using terms as givens when they are not shared referents with the reader. The use of jargon or technical terms whose meanings are unknown to the reader is one of the most common violations of this sort.

The second type of violation occurs when the new element is not clearly related to the given. The logical transition from given to new cannot be too abrupt or, most importantly, cannot be contrary to the reader's expectations without clear justification. To use the example above, even though the image of a person's voice trembling and being low is a shared referent, if the next statement is "showing that he was quite happy," the reader will balk. In this instance, the flow of logic from the given to the new is interrupted. If the writer supplies additional information, such as that the low and trembling voice is characteristic of the client when experiencing strong emotion, the flow will not be interrupted and the contract will not be violated.

The third type of violation occurs when the new information isn't clearly explained or isn't unique. This type of violation can arise in several contexts. When the new information is actually old information, little harm is done. When the new information contradicts expectations or is inconsistent with other information, however, additional explanations are needed.

A special instance of this type of violation occurs when the new is made to appear informative, but is in fact so vague or general that little or no new information is imparted. An example of this type of statement is, "She is a person who is concerned about her feelings." This statement is both vague and true of nearly everyone. This category of given-new contract violation is referred to variously as the *Barnum effect* or as an *Aunt Fanny statement* (Klopfer, 1960; Tallent, 1976). Barnum statements are often overly general, while Aunt Fanny statements are universally true, so that anyone can say it is also true about "my Aunt Fanny."

Understanding the three major categories of violations of the given-new contract will help you make sense out of much of the research on reader satisfaction with psychological reports. This topic is considered further in chapter 4. First, however, it is necessary to review several other basic ideas about written English.

How to Write Intelligibly

Considering written English from the point of view of the given-new contract leads to a general formula for writing intelligibly.

1. *Be sure that the given element in the sentence is a shared referent.* This requires that you carefully consider the person for whom you are writing the report. In writing a report for another psychologist, reporting Wechsler scale or MMPI scores and drawing inferences directly from them may be appropriate. On the other hand, in writing for someone who is not familiar with psychological testing, it may be necessary to provide more explanation. Statements such as "Andrea's performance on a subtest requiring that she quickly assemble puzzles of common objects . . . ," or "Persons who obtain this score are often seen by others as feeling sad, 'blue,' or depressed" convey images that are probably shared experiences with your reader. A writer can be fairly certain that most readers know what puzzles are and what assembling them involves. Similarly, most people know how someone who feels "blue" behaves.

2. *Be sure that the relationship between the given (shared referent) and the new is clear.* An abrupt or illogical transition from the given to the new element will confuse the reader. The flow from the shared referent or given to the new data provided by the report must be unmistakably clear. If the new information is unexpected or appears contradictory to other information, additional explanations may be required.

3. *Be sure that information presented as new is in fact both new and meaningful.* Repeated presentations of broad or generally true statements can create a report that gives a false sense of having communicated important information about a client. In addition to being an extremely poor assessment practice, it is not in the client's best interest for you to make vague statements. It is likely, for example, that readers will find recommendations based on such statements ill founded and unpersuasive.

Repeated violations of the implicit agreement between writer and reader to honor the given-new contract will annoy or confuse the reader and should be avoided. Throughout the book, it is assumed that if you stop to think, you can make a good guess about the referents you share with your readers. It is also possible to systematically assess readers' knowledge of terms that might be used (Ownby & Wallbrown, 1983). When you are unsure, it is a good idea to provide additional explanation. Logical transitions between given and new elements, however, are a more complex issue and are discussed further in the next section.

Sentences

You may recall from classes in elementary school that a sentence can be defined as "a group of words that expresses a complete thought." What the teacher didn't explain, however, was how to tell whether a complete thought had been expressed. Usually, you were left to "feel" whether it was true. Grammarians define a sentence as consisting of a subject and predicate. Presumably, if both are present, a complete, although potentially illogical, thought is expressed. This definition is easier to make operational.

Imagine reading the following sentence outside the context of a report:

The child   /   gazed out the window.

Thinking back to your lessons in prescriptive grammar, you may recall that the phrase "The child" is the subject and "gazed out the window" is the predicate. The sentence works as a grammatical example, but chances are you don't feel that you've been told anything important about a particular child.

Take, for example, the case of Joey Brown, an 11-year-old in Ms. Taylor's fifth-grade class, referred for not paying attention in class and not completing class work. Note how much more vivid the following sentence is:

Joey Brown   /   gazed out the window.

Why is it more vivid? You might answer correctly that it is more specific, but a more compelling reason for its vividness is that "the child" was at best a vaguely shared referent: my idea of "the child" and yours are probably different. On the other hand, both of our concepts of "Joey Brown" include a number of elements, such as the facts that he's 11, a boy, in Ms. Taylor's class, and referred for evaluation because of inattention. In other words, Joey is a shared referent.

To generalize from this example, the subject of a sentence corresponds to the given of the given-new contract. The new, then, is the predicate, the part of the sentence that provides additional information about the given. If you were a reader of the sentence about Joey, you probably knew something about him at the outset, but until you were told, you didn't know the possibly important fact that he gazed out the window during class.

Most declarative sentences in psychological reports are more complex than this example, but they follow the same basic structure. This leads to the following formula: *to write an intelligible sentence in a report, say something new about a shared referent.* Consider this example, which might appear in a report about Joey Brown:

Joey achieved an IQ score of 118.

Here, the given, "Joey," has been established previously in the report by placing his first and last names at the top of the report, probably along with other identifying information. The psychologist also may have explained why finding out Joey's IQ was worth the trouble of administering the test in the Reason for Referral section of the report. The new (something the reader didn't know, but was interested in finding out) is that his IQ is 118. The writer of this sentence has started with something shared with the reader—knowledge of Joey—and told the reader something new about him. Notice how this seemingly simple example follows the prescribed elements of the contract. The given is truly a shared referent, the link is logical because it is quite reasonable that a child should obtain an IQ score when administered an IQ test, and the new information is specific and unique.

Here is an example for practicing the skill of linking sentence elements. The shared referent continues to be Joey; additional information is provided for you to create a declarative statement that consists of a given and a new.

GIVEN: Joey Brown

NEW: Standard score on a reading achievement test = 85

One construction from these two elements might be: "Joey achieved a standard score on a reading achievement test of 85."

Here is another example for practice:

GIVEN: Joey Brown

NEW: Poor performance on geometric drawing task.

A construction from these elements might be: "Joey's performance on a geometric drawing task was poor." Additional practice examples are provided in Appendix A.

Although it might be possible to write a report that consists only of these simple declarative sentences, each containing just one given and one new element, the result would be dull or monotonous writing. Rather than simply putting a string of declarative sentences on paper, most writers vary sentence length so that what is written is more interesting to the reader. For example, you might want to vary sentence length by adding a second related fact to the first in reporting Joey's IQ.

GIVEN: Joey Brown

NEW: He achieved an IQ score of 118.

NEW: An IQ score of 118 is in the high average range of general intellectual ability.

Various grammatical constructions can be used to make writing less monotonous. Although there are more precise terms for such constructions, they can generally be thought of as expressing some type of relationship between two or more ideas. A common way of combining two ideas is the *absolute construction* that allows *coordination* between them:

Joey achieved an IQ score of 118, showing that he is probably functioning in the high average range of general intellectual ability.

In this construction, two ideas have been linked by the word *showing*. Also note that a second given-new sequence is present. This time, the given, *he*, refers to Joey and the new is the statement about high average intellectual function. This type of construction indicates the equivalence of the two elements. Other relationships are indicated by other constructions, such as *contrast* (for example, "She did well on Test A *but* poorly on Test B) or *elaboration* ("She did well on Test A *and* Test B").

Try using contrast with the following given-new elements:

GIVEN: Joey Brown

NEW: High average intellectual function

NEW: Low average reading achievement

One way of relating these two contradictory new elements would be to contrast them by writing "Joey scored in the high average range of general intellectual ability, but in the low average range in reading achievement."

Try using elaboration with these elements:

GIVEN: Joey Brown

NEW: Poor performance on geometric drawings

NEW: Illegible handwriting

Here again, a simple way of relating these elements through elaboration would be to write, "Joey performed poorly on a geometric drawing task, and his handwriting was illegible."

Mastering the process of writing declarative sentences is central to expository writing, which is what psychological reports are all about. Three important relations between given and new elements have been demonstrated: (a) equivalence via the absolute construction, (b) contrast, and (c) elaboration.

Paragraphs

A report cannot consist of a series of short declarative sentences alone, nor can it consist of just one long sentence. Written English is organized into groups of related sentences called *paragraphs*. Paragraphs allow information to be sorted into higher-level units of meaning that contain a series of logically related sentences. You may recall from your previous instruction in writing that a paragraph often contains a *topic sentence* supported by a number of other sentences. Using the framework provided by the given-new contract to consider paragraphs, the topic sentence can be defined as a given-new statement in which the new is phrased generally and requires substantiation. This definition can be clarified with an example.

Suppose that you are engaged in a political discussion with a friend about the relative merits of candidate Bombast. You might begin by saying "Bombast is the best person for the office," but, noticing the dubious look on your friend's face, you decide to furnish substantiating details. You might add, "Bombast is for mom, apple pie, and progressive social legislation," and perhaps even attempt to clinch your argument by saying, "Bombast is for pay raises for psychologists." In this case, you've begun with a given-new statement in which the new is phrased generally ("Bombast is the best person for the office") and substantiated with details (Bombast's positions on the issues).

This point can be illustrated further by the results of Joey's assessment. Suppose that several measures of general intellectual ability have been administered because determination of Joey's intellectual abilities is an important issue for those who are working with him—perhaps there is a question about lateralized brain dysfunction, his ability to profit from verbal psychotherapy, or his eligibility for special education services in the schools. You plan a paragraph in your report on Joey's intellectual ability as estimated by the Wechsler Intelligence Scale for Children–Revised (WISC-III), the Peabody Picture Vocabulary Test–Revised (PPVT-R, measuring receptive vocabulary), and the Raven's Progressive Matrices (Raven's, measuring nonverbal reasoning abilities).

Using the psycholinguistic framework for paragraph construction, you would begin with a statement about Joey's abilities that includes a given and a generally phrased new that requires substantiation: "Joey's test scores show that he is probably functioning in the high average range of general intellectual ability." The given is Joey, and the generally phrased new is the description of his overall level of intellectual functioning. This statement can now be substantiated by a series of given-new sequences that detail test results. Note that in these sequences the given becomes the tests administered (with which the reader is already familiar), and the new elements are the test results. The final product might be:

> Joey's test scores show that he is probably functioning in the high average range of general intellectual ability. His scores on the WISC-III suggest this because his Verbal IQ was 116, his Performance IQ was 120, and his Full Scale IQ was 118. His scores on the PPVT-R and the Raven's tend to confirm these estimates, as they were at standard scores of 114 and 119, respectively. It is thus unlikely that low intellectual abilities account for his academic difficulties.

The last sentence, beginning "It is thus likely . . . ," illustrates one other component of a well-constructed paragraph. This is a summary sentence that draws a conclusion, relates the paragraph's meaning to the referral, provides a link to the next paragraph, or accomplishes a combination of these functions.

Although writing a paragraph within these guidelines may seem awkward at first, it can become natural with practice. Two examples follow. Each brief sentence contains test data related to a particular point. The task is to write a generally phrased given-new sequence as the first sentence of each paragraph, put the data into proper relation (using elaboration, coordination, or contrast), and write a summary sentence to conclude each paragraph.

Example I. Paul is a 32-year-old man referred for evaluation of apparent depression:

1. Paul's scores on the Minnesota Multiphasic Personality Inventory (MMPI) were significantly high on scales 2 (depression) and 7 (agitated anxiety).
2. Paul's responses to questions were brief and tended to express despair and hopelessness.
3. Paul's score on the Beck Depression Inventory (BDI) was 35, usually interpreted as representing "severe" depression.
4. Paul's movements were slow.

Here is one way to combine these ideas into a paragraph:

Results of this assessment indicate that Paul is severely depressed. Results of the MMPI, for example, show that he is probably experiencing feelings of sadness and despair. The results of the BDI also indicate that he is depressed because Paul's score on this measure usually is interpreted as reflecting severe depression. Observation of Paul during testing confirms this impression. His movements were slow and his responses to questions were brief and full of despair and hopelessness. Overall, it appears quite clear that Paul is severely depressed.

Example II. Michelle is a 14-year-old girl referred for evaluation of acting-out behavior at school and at home:

1. Michelle's scores on the Personality Inventory for Children (PIC) were significantly elevated on the DEP (Depression) scale.
2. Michelle's behavior during testing alternated between defiant uncooperativeness and crying.

3. The referring source, a local family psychiatrist, reports that Michelle's parents were recently divorced and that Michelle continues to live with her mother.
4. Michelle's teacher reports that, until recently, she has been an exemplary student and that she has never been a behavior problem before.
5. An interview with Michelle's mother suggests that Michelle may blame her mother for her parents' divorce.

Here is one way to organize this information into a paragraph:

Results of this assessment show that Michelle's acting-out behavior may stem from her anger about her parent's divorce, to which she has reacted by becoming depressed. Several data sources support this idea—Michelle's score on the DEP scale of the PIC was significantly elevated, which suggests that she is experiencing feelings of sadness. Her behavior during testing ranged from defiant uncooperativeness to crying, again suggesting both depression and anger. Finally, an interview with Michelle's mother suggests that Michelle may blame her mother for her parents' divorce and that her acting-out behavior could be an attempt to gain revenge. Therefore, it is unlikely that Michelle's behavior represents a long-standing pattern of maladaptive behavior, but, rather, is a reaction to a current life event.

Organization of Paragraphs in the Report

Ultimately, the paragraphs constructed in this way must be combined into the coherent entity of the full report. Most report writers organize paragraphs into the larger sections of the report outline. These sections give the report a logical flow from referral question to recommendations. Sections usually included are Reason for Referral, Background Information, Assessment Results, and Summary and Recommendations. This organizational scheme gives the report a sequential flow that follows the steps in the evaluation process so that the reader can mentally recreate the process by which the writer reaches the conclusions stated in the report. Paragraphs within these sections follow a similar sequential format and list data in logical order. The precise way in which data are presented, however, depends on the report format. These issues are discussed in detail in chapter 7.

The next chapter considers specific problems in report writing and presents solutions to these problems in the form of an expanded psycholinguistic model for report writing.

Summary

This chapter has reviewed several important issues for you to consider when writing reports. Remember that written and spoken English are different in ways that are important for you to take into account when writing reports. One way to keep these differences in mind is to focus on the given-new contract. If most of the sentences in your report begin with a given element that the reader understands and continue with important new information, you will have made substantial progress in writing better reports. If you can continue with the given-new contract as you write paragraphs and larger sections of the report, you will make even more progress in this direction. The next chapter continues with the psycholinguistic approach to report writing. It considers specific problems in report writing and presents solutions to these problems in the form of an expanded psycholinguistic model for report writing.

4

THE EXPOSITORY PROCESS MODEL

The given-new contract provides a conceptual tool for understanding how to communicate with your reader, and specific guidance about how to write sentences and paragraphs. In this chapter, the problems listed at the end of chapter 2 are reexamined in light of the given-new contract. This review introduces the expository process model (EPM), which applies the psycholinguistic approach to report writing problems. The EPM also gives a specific prescription for how to write good reports.

Language Use Problems

Language use problems arise when the given-new contract is violated. This can happen in several ways. The given may not be mutually understood, the given element may not be logically related to the new, and the new may not be specific or understandable. For example, one important usage problem found in the earlier review of research is that reports often contain terms whose meanings are unclear. Make sure that your readers understand the terms you use in reports. One psychologist tried using the questionnaire developed by Ownby and Wallbrown (Ownby & Wallbrown, 1983) to get feedback about his reports. He discovered, to his surprise, that a teacher with many years of experience did not understand the phrase *visual-motor skills.* The moral here is not to assume that readers will understand technical terms, even when they are elementary to you.

The psychologist above had assumed that *visual-motor skills* was a referent he shared with the teacher and that he could use it without further explanation. Actually, it needed more explanation. The phrase could have been linked to a concrete description, a solution suggested by studies reviewed in chapter 2. The psychologist could have said "Veronica's visual-motor skills were assessed as her ability to copy geometric designs with pencil and paper." The term visual-motor skills is linked to a clear description, and the term becomes a shared referent rather than jargon.

A similar problem concerns using test scores in reports. Psychologists often assume that a score such as the widely used intelligence quotient (IQ) means the same thing to everyone, including lay persons. Rucker (1976b) found that discussion of basic statistical concepts central to intelligence assessment, such as standard error of measurement or confidence intervals, will reveal disagreement among lay persons and probably even among psychologists.

Explaining test scores and tests can be difficult, but with ingenuity it is possible. A drawing with the normal curve on which tests scores can be plotted simplifies explanation of IQ scores and their associated confidence intervals. You can also emphasize the meaning of specific test scores (and their inherent ambiguity) by reporting and interpreting percentile ranks and ranges of scores. What tests measure can be reported by providing a functional explanation of tests and subtests. Subtests from the Wechsler scales, for example, can be described as explaining the meanings of words (Vocabulary) or putting together puzzles of common objects (Object Assembly). Other examples of how to describe tests are given in Appendix C.

Research on reports shows that readers often want raw data from the assessment included in the report, but they also want the data interpreted. Linking assessment data, such as test scores or behavioral observations, to conclusions and recommendations requires that you use terms such as *visual-motor skills* or *depression*. These terms will be jargon without meaning for your readers, however, if they are not shared referents. To avoid this language use problem, make sure that your readers are familiar with the psychological terms used in your report. When you are unsure about your reader's knowledge, always link a description with the term.

Content Problems

Most content problems with reports result from disagreements about the purpose of the report. Studies have shown, for example, that some psychiatrists view specific therapeutic recommendations as inappropriate content, while teachers criticize reports that do not provide specific recommendations. This again highlights the importance of assessing the context into which the report will be sent. This assessment, which should include finding out the needs of the referral source, is discussed extensively in chapter 6.

Failure to consider the report's intended reader might lead psychologists to present an unbalanced picture of the client. Studies show that the types of information given can influence readers' attitudes toward clients and can even affect whether the reader believes that he or she can intervene effectively with the client. These studies show that psychologists should describe not only a client's weaknesses but also his or her strengths. The reader is likely to feel more competent in dealing with the client if the report discusses specific strategies for intervention. The given-new contract, in the realm of content problems, requires an agreement between reader and writer about what should and should not be included in the report. Depending on your assessment of the report's context, as discussed in chapter 6, the contract will not be violated if the report provides a full and balanced description of the client and detailed recommendations about how to help him or her.

It is assumed that the given element—what the assessor and the report's recipients have in common—is the client. The new element is the assessment information. Therefore, the report's organizational format should clearly establish the given, provide relevant information about the assessment's context and purpose, explain assessment results in a way that the reader will understand, and provide succinct conclusions coupled with a suggested course of action. Finally, the information contained in these sections must flow logically toward the summary and recommendations.

Organizational Problems

Few studies have addressed organizational problems in reports, perhaps because they are minor in comparison to other difficulties. It's worth noting, for example, that studies by Pryzwansky and Hanania (1986) and Wiener (1985, 1987; Wiener & Kohler, 1986) showed that the traditional report format is preferred by many consumers in educational settings. Results of this study are confirmed when the given-new distinction is applied at this level of organization. The dictates of the contract allow writers to determine what sort of organization will be most effective for each report.

Purpose of the Report

As the purpose of the report is to provide credible and persuasive statements about clients, consistently honoring the given-new contract can dramatically affect the extent to which the report's purpose is achieved. Statements in the report that do not follow the given-new contract are unlikely to be either credible or persuasive because they will be hard to understand. A report composed of such statements probably would not result in the desired attitude or behavior change.

The Expository Process Model

Research findings and authorities' recommendations seem contradictory. Jargon should be avoided in report writing, but basic assessment data should be included. Terms such as *visual-motor skills* or *depression* must be used to explain basic assessment data, but they may be considered jargon. The writer faces the problem of reporting assessment in a way that includes data but excludes common ways to explain what the data mean.

Some might view this as simply the problem of writing well, but closer scrutiny shows that the answer is not so simple. The problem of jargon in reports is not only a question of using particular words, but also a question of the fundamental process of relating basic data to conclusions. Psychologists accomplish this by integrating their assessment within an implicit theory of cognitive abilities or personality function. They then report the assessment in terms of this theory. For example, the psychologist who believes that the structure of human intellectual abilities can best be understood as one central ability, g, might not emphasize differences between Verbal and Performance IQs on the Wechsler scales in reporting results of intelligence tests. By contrast, the neuropsychologist may view such differences as indications of relative impairment of one of the cerebral hemispheres. In this case, he or she probably will stress the presence of a Verbal–Performance discrepancy in the report.

The problem with the way in which psychologists report assessments is not in their use of professional terms (often called jargon), but rather, in their failure to make explicit the relationship between the underlying theory (in psychological terms) and the data on which the report is based. It is this problem that the expository process model addresses. By clarifying the relationship between the assessment data and the psychologist's interpretation of them, the model helps psychologists to use their theories more effectively in reporting. The model requires that the writer make the relationship between assessment data and terms used in his or her theory explicit and that both of these elements be related logically to the recommendations and conclusions contained within the report. A key term used in the model is *middle-level construct*, first introduced by Appelbaum (1970). The next section explains in detail what middle-level constructs are, as a preliminary to presenting the model itself.

Middle-Level Constructs

In a classic article, Appelbaum (1970) discusses how the writer relates assessment data to conclusions when reporting an evaluation:

> When making inferences, the tester observes individual behaviors, moves to higher levels of abstraction as he connects observations, and moves down again to more data in order to check and extend his inferences—all these steps being guided by his theory. (p. 352)

In this context, *theory* refers not only to whether the psychologist is psychodynamically or behaviorally oriented, but also to the less abstract concepts that he or she invokes in order to explain the client's behavior. While these constructs are often related to higher-level theoretical allegiances, they may be related equally often to the elemental constructs with which the psychologist thinks about the client's ability structure or emotional functioning. Appelbaum calls these terms *middle-level constructs*, lying as they do between the lowest level of raw assessment data and the highest abstraction of formal theory.

Middle-level constructs are probably the very jargon for which reports are criticized. Examples of middle-level constructs are such terms as *intelligence, perceptual skills, anxiety*, or *neurosis*. They are terms that are commonly used in explanations of clients' behavior, but that often do not have a precise shared definition. You can imagine, for example, asking 100 psychologists to define the term *intelligence*. It's likely that they would give you 100 definitions (at least!). Middle-level constructs are useful because they give psychologists a set of terms for communicating with each other. Without the term *intelligence*, it might be difficult or awkward to discuss individual differences in problem-solving skills, even though psychologists often disagree about what *intelligence* really is. Because they mean different things to different persons, middle-level constructs can easily become jargon, or meaningless terms, when they are used in psychological reports without due care to prevent violations of the given-new contract.

It is also possible to see that these constructs can be useful in moving back and forth through the more abstract steps between data and conclusions described by Appelbaum because they provide the reader with conceptual bridges between each part of the writer's logic. The writer is then confronted, however, with the research findings discussed above, which show that using these terms does not always help the reader to understand, but may, in fact, hinder him or her. How can this paradox be resolved?

One answer lies in the way writers use middle-level constructs. A number of authors, for example, have commented on the need to provide data, such as observations and test responses, within the report as a way of helping the reader understand the writer's conclusions. To cite Appelbaum once again: "By thus offering the reader a sense of underlying data founded on normative experience, the psychologist makes his theoretical remarks less abstruse" (p. 352). Given the need for data within the report and the potential usefulness of middle-level constructs, the possibility emerges that what is wrong with the use of these constructs in reports is not their content—the terms themselves—but their relationship to what the reader already knows (the degree to which they are shared referents) or to the client (the degree to which the middle-level constructs are clearly related to the purpose of the assessment). In terms of the given-new contract, any of the three types of violations can occur when writers use middle-level constructs. The construct can be used as a given when it is not truly a shared referent, the relationship between the given information and a new construct can be unclear, or the construct can be used as a new when its meaning is not at all clear.

Researchers have often demonstrated that reading comprehension is related to prior knowledge of subject matter. (See Entin & Klare, 1985.) This suggests that readers will understand the writer's statements best when they have a background knowledge of what the report is about. Briefly stated, if a middle-level construct is not clearly related to data in the report or to what the reader already knows, it will not be understood. If the middle-level construct has no clear relationship to the purpose of the report in providing conclusions and recommendations about the client, it will be irrelevant and distracting.

The hypothesis that what's wrong with middle-level constructs is not the terms themselves, but how they are used in reports, leads to a model for writing sentences and paragraphs in reports. The expository process model proposes the following rules for using middle-level constructs:

I. *Any middle-level construct in a report must have a directly shared referent in data either implicitly or explicitly contained in the report.*

This statement means that all middle-level constructs used in a report must be clearly related to something both the reader and writer know about. For example, before the writer can make the statement "auditory perceptual skills are poor," he or she must have determined that *auditory perceptual skills* is a phrase that is a shared referent with the report's intended recipient, as might be the case when a psychologist writes a report to a speech pathologist.

If the phrase is not a shared referent, it should be made into one by referencing it to a concrete description. It might be possible to state, for example, that "The client's auditory perceptual skills were assessed as his ability to break words down into their component sounds." In this case, the subsequent statement that these skills are poor has a clear meaning for the reader.

II. *Conclusions are evaluative statements about the middle-level construct and must be supported by data.*

Conclusions are evaluative statements that say something about the degree or extent of the construct. These evaluative statements must also be supported by data in the report. For example, the statement "the client's level of anxiety is significantly high" includes the middle-level construct *anxiety* and the conclusion *is significantly high*. Such a statement, according to the model, must be supported by reference to data. In this case, the reference might be that the client's score on scale 7 of the MMPI was 85, which will produce the following: "The client's level of anxiety is significantly high—her score on scale 7 of the MMPI was a T of 85."

III. *Recommendations must be logically related to conclusions stated in the report.*

This proposal specifies that the recommendations be clearly derived from the construct and the conclusion. Although a recommendation for a psychiatric evaluation might be appropriate for a client, it should not be made in a report if the reason for it has not been established previously. The groundwork for each recommendation, therefore, must be laid in the preceding sections of the report.

These three proposals derive directly from the observation that the reader of the report wants a well-reasoned explanation of how the psychologist arrived at his or her conclusions. Figures 4.1 through 4.4 graphically represent the steps in the model in greater detail. Figure 4.1 illustrates the first step in implementing the model. Results of the assessment provide the raw data on which the report is based. Of course, your choice of assessment instruments implies something about your theoretical orientation and thus the middle-level constructs you are likely to use.

Assessment data can be organized in any way you prefer, but you should probably organize it according to the type of report you plan to write. You might create a formal worksheet, or simply jot down notes to which you can refer when writing the report. If you plan a

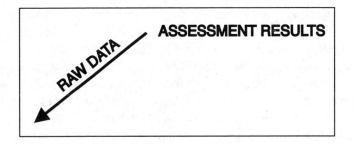

Figure 4.1   The Expository Process Model—Step One: The Assessment Provides Raw Data

In this first step, the assessment results in the raw data on which the report is based.

hypothesis-oriented report, you might make notes about each hypothesis. If the referral question is about a child's academic underachievement, for example, your hypothesis might be that expressive language deficits are a central cause of the child's academic problems. You could make this hypothesis a heading, and then list evidence for and against it. If you plan a domain-oriented report, you could have headings for each domain you plan to describe in the report.

Figure 4.2 illustrates the critical second step in using the model. You must relate the data you have already organized to the middle-level constructs you will invoke to interpret the data for your reader. Several data sources should be cross-referenced to support the middle-level construct. A client's score on the Vocabulary subtest of one of the Wechsler intelligence scales might reflect any of the following: general

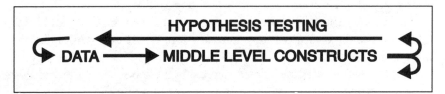

Figure 4.2   The Expository Process Model—Step Two: Hypothesis Testing

In this step, data from the assessment are used to derive hypotheses. In turn, these are tested against other assessment data in a cyclic process.

intellectual ability, general language skills, expressive language skills, degree of acculturation, or educational experiences. Accurate interpretation requires that you find other data that will support the middle-level construct you choose. If this client has a low score on Vocabulary, but high scores on all the Performance subtests of the Wechsler and a high score on the Peabody Picture Vocabulary Test (a measure of vocabulary that does not require expressive language), you might invoke the middle-level construct *expressive language skills*. If the same client is a native speaker of Spanish but is tested in English, degree of acculturation might be implicated.

Figure 4.2 also emphasizes the iterative aspect of this step of the model as you look at data, develop hypotheses about what they mean, and then return to the data to check your hypotheses (as recommended by Appelbaum, 1970, and more recently by Lerner, 1990). When you note the client's low score on the Vocabulary test, for example, you might initially hypothesize that the client has poor language skills generally. The middle-level construct *general language skills* would thus be supported. You would then return to the data to test your hypothesis. You might note the high scores on all the Performance subtests—this would support the middle-level construct *language skills* and move your interpretation away from "general intellectual ability." So far, so good. You then would move to other data, and note the high score on the Peabody Picture Vocabulary Test. This score presents a problem for the middle-level construct *general language skills*, since in the back of your mind you are probably thinking ahead to the next step when you evaluate the middle-level construct. Since the data do not show that all language skills are poor, you return to the middle-level construct. What middle-level construct is consistent with the data? If not *general* language skills, what about *expressive* language skills? You have just formulated a modified hypothesis. You now return to the data, and find that, yes, the data support this modification. Other data will be interpreted similarly.

Figure 4.3 illustrates the last steps in using the model. In it the middle-level constructs are now evaluated. Inherent in using the middle-level construct is an observation about its status—whether cognitive skills are good or bad, or whether psychotic thought processes are paranoid or disorganized. The next step in the model is to evaluate the middle-level construct and to create a *causal link* to the referral question by

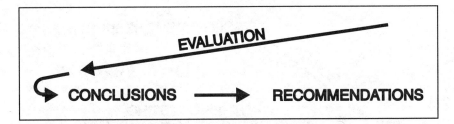

Figure 4.3   The Expository Process Model—Step Three: Drawing Conclusions and Making Recommendations

In this step, middle-level constructs are evaluated and related to conclusions. Recommendations are made based on these evaluations.

stating a *conclusion*. Perhaps the client discussed above was referred because of academic underachievement in college. If you invoke the middle-level construct *expressive language skills*, you might *evaluate* them as below average. The *conclusion* you would draw in this sequence would then be: "The client is doing poorly in his college English class because of below average expressive language skills." This interpretation might be contrasted with the client's performance on measures of mathematics skills, especially if he is doing well in a college algebra class. Conclusions should then be linked to recommendations. Again, there should be a *causal link* between conclusion and recommendation. To continue the example, you might recommend that the client be given special tutoring in English, or referred for language therapy.

You can test the relationship between the conclusion and referral question, or between the recommendation and the conclusion, by asking the question "Why?" Working backward through the example, ask "Why provide tutoring?" If you cannot answer this question based on data in the report, you have not provided a causal link. In the example, the answer to this question would be, "Because the client's expressive language skills are below average and he is doing poorly in his English class." To test the causal link between the conclusion and the referral question, ask "Why is the client doing poorly in his English class?" Here the answer would be "Because his expressive language skills are below average." Figure 4.4 presents an integrated overview of the entire expository process model.

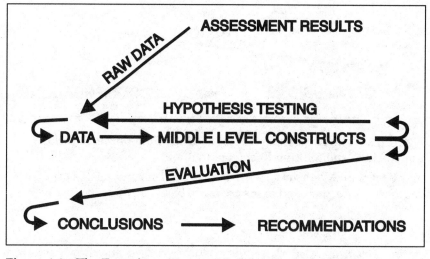

Figure 4.4   The Expository Process Model—Final Step: The Complete Model

It should be noted that these steps do not have to be immediately contiguous within the report. Data can be presented in one section, middle-level constructs in another, conclusions presented in yet another, and recommendations appended as a list at the end of the report. What is critical is that the constituents logically follow each other and that their relationship is apparent to the reader. In many cases, it is best to place raw data and constructs together because the construct is usually a significant abstraction from the data, and clarity may require that this relationship be understood easily.

Examples may help to illustrate how the model can be applied and the benefits that can result from developing better sentences. Here is an example of a nonmodel statement that begins with a middle-level construct:

> Visual-motor skills are poor, and work on remedial tasks such as puzzles and tracing is recommended.

Analyzing this example according to the model, a middle-level construct (visual-motor skills) is presented with a conclusion (they are poor) and a recommendation (use puzzles and tracing). The absence of elaboration of the middle-level construct prevents elaboration of the conclusion and recommendation because without supporting data, a highly specific recommendation such as "use puzzles" is not obviously needed. Although the recommendation follows logically, it is not immediately clear to the reader in what way working with puzzles or tracing may help in developing visual-motor skills. A causal link has not been created.

Contrast the first example with the following model-based one:

The client had difficulty with several tasks, such as copying drawings and putting together puzzles of common objects. These difficulties suggest the client has poor visual-motor skills and that work on tracing tasks and putting together puzzles may help her develop these skills.

Analyzing this example shows that its elements include, in sequence, data (copying drawings and putting together puzzles), a middle-level construct (visual-motor skills), a conclusion (they are poor) and the same recommendation as in the first example (use tracing tasks and puzzles).

Here is another example of a nonmodel statement:

The client appears depressed, and it is recommended that he be seen by a psychotherapist.

Here is the model-based equivalent:

The client's behavior during assessment, which included frequent sighs, rare smiles, and crying, suggests that he is depressed. It is recommended that he be seen by a psychotherapist.

Once again, the model-based statement is more vivid and communicates the psychologist's message in a more concrete and easily understandable fashion.

Studies of the EPM (Ownby, 1984; 1990a, 1990b) show that various groups of report consumers (a group of parents and educational specialists in Ownby, 1984) and persons who write reports (clinical and counseling psychologists in Ownby, 1990a; school psychologists in Ownby, 1990b) rated model-based statements as significantly more credible and persuasive than similar statements that were not based on the model. EPM-based statements are longer than the simpler statements they are compared with here. Sentence length, rather than the logical structure imposed by the model, might account for these ratings. Follow-up analysis of the data in these three studies was done after publication of the referenced papers. These analyses showed that the effects that caused higher ratings for model-based statements could be separated into components due to sentence length and those due to sentence structure. The effect of the model remained significant after the component of sentence length was removed from the analysis. The logical relations among data, middle-level constructs, conclusions, and recommendations are clarified by the structure imposed by the model. This clarification results in important differences in how readers view the statements.

Advantages of using the model for report writing are that it provides a clear structure for writing effective statements and that it can be used by psychologists independent of their theoretical orientation. Expository process model-based statements are, by definition, data-based and logical because the structure of the model ensures that the logical argument in the statement proceeds step by step from data to conclusions. There is nothing magical about the model, of course, but it does provide a specific formula for implementing the recommendations of a number of experts on how to use data and technical terms in reports.

The Model with Paragraphs

At a more complex level, the model can be used to build statements at progressively higher levels of abstraction from data, whether the writer is building from several bits of data or from several already supported middle-level constructs. The schematic for this more complex organization is suggested in Figure 4.5.

This diagram presents the possible macrostructure of model-based reports. Various types and quantities of data, depending on their distinctiveness (as in the case of behavioral observations) or validity and departure from the norm (as in the case of test scores) may be used to infer middle-level constructs. One data element may lead to one construct and one resulting conclusion and recommendation (line 1). Lines 2 to 4 of Figure 4.5 present progressively more complex instances of the possible relationships of data to middle-level constructs, conclusions, and recommendations. It can be seen, for example, that several

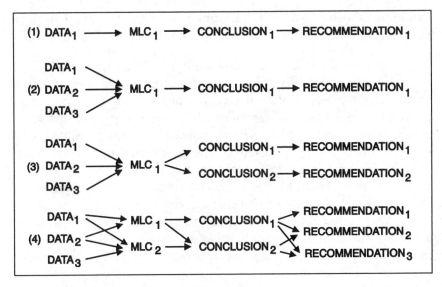

Figure 4.5   Data Sequences in the EPM

bits of data may contribute to the different constructs, one construct can contribute to several conclusions, and that other, even more complex combinations are possible.

Construct-conclusion sequences also can stand alone when their implications for the client's situation are obvious (for example, if the sequence were "abilities are normal"), or they may lead to higher-order conclusions, which can include an evaluative constituent and other explanations that make the conclusions more understandable to the reader.

Again, examples can serve to clarify these points. Here is part of a set of data obtained during the evaluation of a school-age child:

1. John made impulsive errors in sight word recognition;
2. John's scaled score on the Digit Span subtest of the WISC-III was 6; Coding was 4; Arithmetic was 6;
3. John's classroom teacher reports that he is more impulsive and active than his classmates;
4. John's principal reports that he is defiant of authority;
5. John's teachers report that he often does not respond to their requests;

6. John's scores on a behavior rating scale indicate that he displays an unusual amount of acting-out behavior.

Data from statements 1 to 3 could be used to infer the middle-level construct *attentional skills deficits*, which, in turn, could lead to a conclusion of the presence of *attention-deficit/hyperactivity disorder*. Such a conclusion could lead to recommendations for cognitive behavior modification interventions, medical evaluation for the possible use of stimulant medication, and perhaps special tutoring in reading skills. Data from statements 4 to 6 might lead to the inference *problems in impulse control*, which by itself could lead to recommendations for behavioral treatment. Note also that a conclusion, as intended in the model, can consist only of an evaluative statement about the nature of a middle-level construct, as with *problems in impulse control*. In this case, the logical flow to recommendations is understandable to the reader without further discussion.

Depending on the severity of the problem, however, and on other factors, some psychologists might go further and infer the presence of *conduct disorder*, a conclusion that might lead to recommendations about classroom management, family counseling, or special class placement. Note also that while the conclusion is still evaluative it can include the inference of a disorder's presence.

Recalling the definition of a paragraph from chapter 3, it is now possible to apply the model to writing paragraphs. That definition stated that paragraphs consist of three elements:

1. a *topic sentence* that includes a given-new sequence in which the new is phrased generally and requires substantiation;
2. several *given-new sequences* that provide substantiation of the new in the topic sentence; and
3. a *final statement* that summarizes the paragraph, relates its meaning to the referral question, provides flow to the next paragraph, or some combination of these.

In terms of the model, the generally phrased new element in the topic sentence could be a middle-level construct whose relevance to the client's functioning is clarified through assessment data. In this discussion, paragraphs with this sort of structure will be referred to as Type I. An example follows:

This assessment suggests that Sybil is depressed. She often sighed and occasionally cried during test administration. When asked, she acknowledged feeling a negative mood and said she often feels "What's the use?" Her scores on the MMPI reflect this as well. Her T score of 82 on scale 2 is often interpreted as reflecting a significant feeling of negativism and low mood. Taken together, these results indicate the presence of functionally significant depression, which is at least a partial explanation for her recent poor work and school performance.

The phrase "Sybil is depressed" is element one, the topic sentence, and details such as "T score of 82" are the second element, given-new sequences that substantiate the topic sentence. The last sentence is the third element, the final summary statement.

Here is another example:

These results show that John is probably suffering from a significant anxiety disorder. His own description of his concerns, which include feelings of panic and terror, is consistent with this idea. Observations of him during an episode of severe anxiety are also consistent— he was clearly agitated, was trembling, and was difficult to communicate with at the time. These results show that his concerns probably arise from an anxiety disorder rather than a heart condition, especially because his physician reports that the latter condition is not present.

It may be helpful for you to try to determine which elements in this paragraph correspond to the three elements of the Type I paragraph.

An alternative way of structuring the paragraph is to present a general statement in the topic sentence that leads to the middle-level construct at the end of the paragraph. This structure, called Type II, is useful when the middle-level construct deserves special emphasis. An example follows:

Jacob's school performance suggests that his difficulties may stem from either low general ability or poor academic skills. His IQ scores on the WISC-III (Verbal IQ = 123; Performance IQ = 125; Full Scale IQ = 124), as well as his standard score equivalent on the PPVT-R (128), suggest that he functions in the superior range of general intellectual ability. By contrast, his academic achievement test scores on the Woodcock-Johnson Psycho-Educational Battery are much lower (Reading cluster standard score = 87; Mathematics = 83; Written Language = 82). These results suggest that Jacob may present an educationally significant specific learning disorder.

In this case, the focus of the paragraph is on the middle-level construct *specific learning disorder*. It is positioned at the end of the paragraph for special emphasis because it is important new information about the child's functioning.

To summarize the elements of the two types of paragraphs:

Type I: 1. A *topic sentence* that includes a middle-level construct
2. *Data*
3. A *conclusion*, which usually summarizes and explains the functional significance of the findings

Type 2: 1. A *topic sentence* without a middle-level construct
2. *Data*
3. A *conclusion* that includes and emphasizes a middle-level construct

Remember that the model stresses, first, the importance of establishing a particular kind of logical sequence in a report sentence or paragraph. The report should move from a given, which provides the reader with a conceptual anchor, to the new information provided by the writer. Second, the model stresses the importance of referencing all middle-level constructs to data.

Examine the two types of paragraph structure from the point of view of the model. You can see that the Type I structure establishes a given-new sequence in its topic sentence. The data to which the model is tied follow it immediately as substantiation for the sequence. At a higher organizational level, Type I structure supports the higher-level given-new sequence in the report's sections by moving from the Referral Question to Recommendations sections and, thus, relates the paragraph's meaning to the sections of the report that follow it. The properly constructed paragraph establishes information that creates a new shared referent, or given. This given can then be related to the new elements that follow it, such as additional assessment data, conclusions, or recommendations.

The Type II structure also follows the model's format. Here, the middle-level construct is not included in the topic sentence. The function of the topic sentence in this paragraph is only to establish the given. In this type of structure, all the new information is in the body of the paragraph that follows the given in the topic sentence. Data that follow the topic sentence lead to the concluding sentence in the paragraph that contains the middle-level construct.

This structure allows the writer to emphasize the middle-level construct by inducing a minor degree of uncertainty in the reader, who is provided with data and reasoning, but not the actual conclusion until the end of the paragraph. This type of paragraph can be thought of as inducing an expectancy in the reader by providing the topic sentence and data; when the conclusion is provided, the expectancy is resolved. The mechanism by which this occurs might be considered the written language equivalent of the more familiar experiments in perception, in which completion of a figure is demonstrated to produce the experience of completion in the viewer. (See Koffka, 1935, pp. 177–210). The use of this type of structure to emphasize what is included at the end also is suggested by Strunk and White (1979, pp. 32–33).

In order to test the predictions of this model about paragraphs, a questionnaire was given to groups of clinical and counseling psychologists (Ownby, 1990a). The questionnaire included two sets of two paragraphs, one Type I and the other Type II structure. Each set of two paragraphs included one that conformed to the model and another that included the same elements, but was organized so that it did not conform to the model. For example, the topic sentence in the nonmodel Type I paragraph was placed in the middle of the paragraph so that it did not establish a given prior to the inclusion of new data. In the nonmodel Type II paragraph, the topic sentence and conclusion were placed together at the beginning of the paragraph so that it mirrored a more typical paragraph organization. Readers indicated that the paragraphs that conformed to the predictions of the model communicated more effectively than the matched nonmodel paragraphs.

Type I structures highlight the functional significance of test findings, while Type II structures emphasize the middle-level construct. In the example above about Sybil, the writer may know that the reader has some general awareness of her difficulties and will be most interested in an explanation of the relationship between her emotional status and work performance. In the example above about the school child, Jacob may have been referred, as such children sometimes are, for behavior problems or emotional disturbance. Stressing the meaning of the middle-level construct in this case is an important way of making sure the reader understands that a problem that is not obvious to the casual observer may be the cause of Jacob's behavior. In the first instance, the larger given-new structure of the complete report is advanced by the conclusion of the paragraph, which establishes Sybil's depression as the reason for her adjustment difficulties; the fact that she is depressed becomes a shared referent between the writer and reader. The writer can then go on to elucidate etiological factors in Sybil's depression. In the second instance, the writer may go on to explain the functional significance of Jacob's learning disorder, in this way again advancing the larger given-new structure of the complete report.

The Model with Sections of the Report

The model may also be applied to sections of the report. In this case, various givens can be connected to their respective new elements either directly or via middle-level constructs. For example, in the Reason for Referral section of the report, you might construct the following Type I paragraph, which emphasizes the data:

> In referring Jacob, Ms. Landsdowne, his first-grade teacher, notes his frequent misbehavior. She reports that "he often talks out in class and acts in a way that is disruptive." Thus, the focus of this assessment was to determine what might account for Jacob's misbehavior in the classroom.

The general middle-level construct here is *misbehavior*, while the substantiating data are quotes from Ms. Landsdowne's referral. The concluding statement summarizes the data and relates the paragraph to the report's overall purpose. In presenting background information, similar paragraphs might be written with concluding sentences that relate the information to the reason for referral.

A common practice is to begin the Assessment Results section of the report with a listing of assessment measures, in this way establishing what sources of information the writer has drawn from in developing the report. Depending on the method of reporting the results—by functional domain or hypotheses about the referral question—the succeeding paragraphs present data from the assessment measures. This structure follows the model by establishing the assessment measures as given elements before it discusses the new information, the assessment results.

The Results section, in turn, usually is followed by a Summary. The first paragraph of the Summary should almost always be structured in Type I format. Its given element should be (a) a phrase such as "Assessment results show . . . ," or (b) a brief restatement of the referral question. This allows the reader to relate the completed narration of assessment results that precede this section to the overall purpose of the assessment. Examples of these two approaches follow, with the given elements in italics:

a. *Assessment results show* that Sybil's work and school difficulties are probably the result of significant depression stemming from her parents' divorce approximately 6 months ago.
b. *The results show* that John is suffering from an anxiety disorder.
c. *Jacob's school behavior difficulties* probably stem from an educationally significant specific learning disorder.

The new element in these statements probably will be anticipated by the reader. The purpose of including this type of statement at this point in the report is to provide the reader with a bridge between the already narrated assessment results and the conclusions contained in the Summary section. In this way, causal links are established.

As in other Type I paragraphs, data that substantiate the generally phrased topic sentence follow, but in the Summary this should consist of a brief review of significant assessment findings already discussed— no new data should be introduced in the Summary. These review statements usually are sentences that relate the middle-level constructs or assessment data introduced in the Assessment Results section. They are now shared referents due to their having been related to data in previous statements. In Sybil's case, the topic sentence provided above could be followed by:

Her behavior during assessment, her reported low mood, and her responses to the MMPI all support this idea.

In John's case:

His complaints of panic and terror, as well as observations of him during an episode, suggest that this conclusion is correct.

In Jacob's case:

> In the absence of other reasons for these difficulties, the severe discrepancy between his scores on measures of ability and achievement supports this idea.

The final sentence in the Summary should always relate the conclusions contained in the Summary to the Recommendations section that will follow it. This sentence should include a given element that refers to the assessment results and a new element that is a general recommendation for a course of action. In Sybil's case, this might be:

> These results indicate that psychotherapeutic interventions should be considered with Sybil.

In John's case:

> These findings suggest the potential usefulness of medical and psychotherapeutic interventions with John.

In Jacob's case:

> These results show that Jacob may be eligible for special educational assistance.

The Recommendations section then follows, perhaps introduced with a generally phrased given-new sequence such as "This assessment suggests that the following recommendations may be helpful to those who are working with this client." After this introduction, detailed recommendations can be listed, such as, "Explore assertiveness training with Sybil" or "Try a linguistic approach to reading instruction with Jacob."

The Model and the Complete Report

This chapter has detailed how the central ideas of the model can be applied to the various types of structural problems in report writing. The model also can be applied to organizational variables in the report; the report format suggested in chapter 7 follows the guidelines of the model and is already used widely. An outline for the overall structure of the report might state briefly the preliminary givens necessary to understanding the report's ultimate conclusions. These would probably include a statement of the client's identifying data, the reason for referral, and the sources of information used in the assessment. The new elements to be discussed include the test results, the middle-level constructs used to explain test results, conclusions, summary, and recommendations. These elements establish the superordinate given elements in the report: the client, the purpose of the assessment, and the assessment tools used. The new elements make the assessment results shared referents with the reader by relating assessment data to middle-level constructs and conclusions. When assessment results become shared referents, the resulting newly created givens can be used to further develop the argument of the overall report into conclusions and recommendations.

The Worksheet

The specificity of the model allows you to construct a report writing worksheet (see Figure 4.6). With this worksheet, you can make model sequences explicit even though raw assessment data, middle-level

Domain	Data	MLC	Conclusion	Recommendation
Cognitive–Academic	1. Impulsive sight word recognition errors	Attention	1. Skills are poor	1. Provide structure in the classroom
	2. WISC-III scores: Arithmetic = 6 Digit Span = 6 Coding = 4	Distractibility	2. Possible attention-deficit/ hyperactivity disorder	2. Provide reading instruction with a "stop and think" approach
	3. Test behavior: Overactive	Impulsivity		3. Refer for medical evaluation for stimulant medication
Behavioral	1. Principal says: "Defiant"	Behavior disturbance	Possible conduct disorder	1. Consider special class placement
	2. Teacher says: "Can't control."			2. Group therapy
	3. Rating scales: "Acting out"			3. Community program for predelinquents

Figure 4.6 An EPM Worksheet

constructs, conclusions, and recommendations may appear in different sections. Note that the worksheet can also be organized by section or report, ability domain, or any other organizing principle you wish.

Once the macrostructure of the report is outlined with the model, the actual writing can proceed easily. After background data and the reason for referral are presented, the content of the report narrative can be drawn directly from the model worksheet. Not all data elements must be written into the body of the report; the writer should draw selected examples from the data column, always using at least one element for each middle-level construct that is linked to a shared referent and keeping in mind the intended recipient's knowledge of the middle-level constructs used in the report.

Additional examples for practice are provided in Appendix A.

Summary

The expository process model is the result of a synthesis of the ideas of psycholinguistic research on the given-new contract in discourse comprehension, Appelbaum's idea of the middle-level construct, and previous research on report writing. Through this synthesis, a model for structuring the elements of the psychological report is provided. This model gives guidance about how to write sentences, paragraphs, and the larger sections of the report. Several studies have shown that sentences and paragraphs written using the model's guidelines are viewed as significantly more credible and persuasive than similar sentences and paragraphs that are not written using these guidelines.

There are several advantages to using the model: (a) it ensures that all statements are data-based, a characteristic recommended by many experts in the field; (b) it clarifies the logical structure of each argument in the report, from raw data to recommendations; (c) it provides a model to guide report writers; and (d) empirical supports show that it may be useful in achieving the goals of report writing. It is not a panacea for the ills of report writing—it will not cure problems in basic knowledge of assessment procedures, nor will it cure problems that arise from an assessment that is poorly organized or thought out. Initially, its use even may appear to make the process of report writing more difficult, but with practice the model can help psychologists write more readable and more useful reports.

5

REPORT MODELS AND LINGUISTIC STYLES

Report *models* and linguistic *styles* are two important issues to consider in writing reports. The way the sections of the report are organized is determined by the report model. Reports, for example, can be organized around functional domains, hypotheses tested in the assessment, or test instruments. The way the writer expresses him- or herself through choices about language is the linguistic style. These two issues are closely related because both model and style depend on deciding how the report will function in its context. The theory of reporting discussed in chapter 1 specifies that organizational variables such as model and style interact with contextual variables: The report's model and style depend on the referral agent, the referral problem, and the environment in which the report will be used.

Providing credible and persuasive statements about clients has already been defined as the purpose of the report. Consideration of the report in its context, however, is necessary to decide which report model should be used. Two models are currently used: *hypothesis-oriented*, in which the report is organized around answers to the referral questions, and *domain-oriented*, in which the report is organized by functional domain. The third model, *test-oriented*, is organized based on a test-by-test description of results, but is not as commonly used.

It is important for psychologists to consider their own beliefs about psychological assessment in choosing a report model. A psychologist with a background in humanistic psychology, for example, might not want to write a test-oriented report because of the belief that this type of report reduces the client to a set of numbers. Another psychologist with training in psychoanalysis may want to organize a psychological report around domains or developmental concepts consistent with his or her training. Many psychologists develop a personal style in report writing in which a particular model is essential. Writers, therefore, may be reluctant to modify their style even when changing it might be desirable. Sometimes, changing style improves the effectiveness of a report when it is tailored for its context.

For example, a report written to a client's psychotherapist might provide, in addition to answers to referral questions, a general description of the client's personality functioning. Here, the psychologist might write a comprehensive domain-oriented report. A forensic psychology report, by contrast, might address a narrow issue, such as a client's competence to stand trial. Here, the psychologist might address only the hypothesis that the client is or is not competent to take part in legal proceedings.

The wishes of the report's intended recipient may also affect model choice. The psychotherapist mentioned above might be interested in the additional data about the client included in the domain-oriented report. A judge or lawyer who read the same report might find the additional material irrelevant.

The relationship of these issues to model choice is considered here. Further discussion of how to tailor the report by professional specialty and theoretical orientation appears in chapter 8.

Report Models

The term *models* primarily refers to the organization by which assessment data are presented in the report. Thus, models are most important to consider in writing the Assessment Results section of the report, though choice of model may also affect the way other sections, such as Reason for Referral or Background Information, are written. The three models to be discussed here are (a) hypothesis-oriented, (b) domain-oriented, and (c) test-oriented. While in practice it might be possible to identify other models, these three can probably be considered representative.

Hypothesis-Oriented

The hypothesis-oriented report provides the reader with a statement or series of statements about the answers the assessment can provide to the referral questions. The remaining sections address specific issues related to the hypotheses by providing model-based paragraphs that communicate assessment results. The following example is drawn from a neuropsychological test report about a woman referred for evaluation of memory difficulties. Because of the report's length, only the first and second paragraphs of the Assessment Results section are reproduced here in order to illustrate how a general hypothesis can be stated and then followed with supporting information.

> Results of this assessment indicate that there are probably multiple sources of Ms. Client's complaints and apparent difficulties. She shows quite obvious mental clouding, difficulties in new verbal learning, motor difficulties suggestive of left cerebral hemisphere dysfunction, and social-emotional difficulties; all of these may be related to her current adjustment problems.
>
> Mental clouding and attentional difficulties were noted on interview with Ms. Client. She has frequent lapses as she speaks, loses her train of thought often, and requires prompting in order for her to remain on the topic . . . this problem alone would make it difficult for Ms. Client to function in any job that requires concentration, even at so rudimentary a level as making mental arithmetic calculations. In this connection, it should be noted that Ms. Client performed particularly poorly on those subtests of the WAIS-R that require short-term memory (Digit Span = 4 forward and 3 backward) and mental problem solving (Arithmetic scaled score = 6, or the 9th percentile). In addition, she performed poorly on a subtest that involves concentration in combination with clerical speed and accuracy (Digit Symbol scaled score = 5, or the 5th percentile). These difficulties are likely to continue to interfere with Ms. Client's ability to function occupationally.
>
> In assessment of her memory difficulties . . .

The report continues with paragraphs that discuss Ms. Client's memory difficulties, possible left cerebral hemisphere dysfunction, and social-emotional difficulties. Each paragraph discusses one of the issues raised in the hypotheses paragraph placed at the beginning of the section. Each paragraph addresses a specific concern raised in the Reason for Referral section. The Summary section then ties together the answers provided in each paragraph and provides an overview of the client's functioning.

Domain-Oriented

The advantages of the domain-oriented model are its comprehensiveness and its ability to communicate a balanced picture of the client's strengths and weaknesses. The writer may organize the results section with or without headings, depending on the complexity and length of the report. Useful headings might be Cognitive Abilities, Academic Achievement, or Personality Functioning. Within the sections defined by these headings, a narrative of test results can be written that focuses on providing a general description of the client and relating test data to the referral question. Paragraphs constructed within the guidelines of the EPM will serve this function.

A potential disadvantage of this model is the possibility of providing the reader with more information than he or she wishes. Use of this model is indicated when the report's intended recipient is likely to be interested in an extended discussion of the client's abilities and personality functioning. This situation might arise when the reason for referral is to obtain a better "general understanding" of the client. This model might also be appropriate when the referral request is vague, and it is not possible to obtain further clarification of the referral agent's wishes with respect to the report. Here, the writer may provide the reader with as much information as is reasonable. The relationship of referral problem to type of assessment and report is discussed further in chapter 6.

Here is an example of a domain-oriented report's Assessment Results section. Headings are used that reflect specific domains of function.

Cognitive abilities. Results of this assessment indicate that Marie is probably functioning in the average range of general intellectual ability (WISC-III Verbal IQ = 103; Performance IQ = 100; Full Scale IQ = 101). When Marie's scores on the subtests of the WISC-III are combined so that they contribute to specific abilities (factor analytically derived deviation quotients), she shows borderline impaired performance on the factor that represents attention, concentration, and control of high-level cognitive processes. This score suggests that Marie may present difficulties in sustaining attention in a large classroom and that her teachers may report that she often must be reminded to pay attention. Other children who score at this level often have academic skills difficulties and specific learning disorders.

Visual-motor abilities. Assessment of Marie's visual-motor abilities as her skill at copying geometric forms with pencil and paper . . .

Academic achievement. Assessment of Marie's reading and math skills (Woodcock-Johnson Psycho-Educational Battery) suggests that while she performs at average levels in the area of reading skills development, she may perform at lower levels in the area of math skills (Reading cluster standard score = 99, or the 48th percentile; Math cluster standard score = 90, or the 26th percentile) . . .

This example shows how the domain-oriented report can provide a complete and thorough understanding of the areas of the client's functioning evaluated during the assessment.

Test-Oriented

In this model, assessment results are presented sequentially by assessment measure used, often with headings such as Wechsler Adult Intelligence Scale–Revised or Minnesota Multiphasic Personality Inventory. Although this model has the advantage of making the sources of assessment data clear, it has little else to recommend it. The emphasis on tests detracts from the overall presentation of the client as a person by drawing attention to specific tests and scores rather than to their relevance to the client's functioning. The emphasis on tests also communicates the impression that psychological assessment consists of giving tests and interpreting them on an individual basis, rather than using multiple information sources in order to arrive at answers to important questions about the client. Although popular in the past, this model is to be avoided.

Each of the report models has advantages and disadvantages. Exclusive use of the hypothesis-oriented model means that occasionally you may not supply the reader with all the information he or she wants. Conversely, exclusive use of the domain-oriented model may mean that you spend time reporting data that the reader doesn't need or want. Ultimately, then, the decision of what report model to use should depend on how the report is to function within the contextual variables.

Linguistic Style

Ownby and Wallbrown (1986) defined style in psychological reports as "the consistent tone of the language of the report defined by vocabulary and the complexity and type of grammatic structure used" (p. 32). This definition implies, first, that the writer of the report makes reasoned decisions about the way he or she uses language in the report. Most writers of psychological reports, for example, avoid slang or idiom because that would be inconsistent with the professional tone of the psychological report. A second implication of this definition is that the writer's decisions are made on a consistent basis over time. The choices of vocabulary and grammatic structure are likely to be the same at the end of the report as at the beginning. Third, this definition divides style into two closely related elements: vocabulary and grammatic structure. This division makes consideration of the types of decisions writers make in producing a report easier. With this definition in mind, it may be useful to consider what experts on report writing have suggested.

Klopfer (1960) provides an early, but still pertinent, discussion of style in psychological reports. He reviews research to the date of his writing and concludes that reports should be written in a style that emphasizes accuracy, integration, readability, clarity, and individuality. Klopfer also stresses the importance of adherence to the rules of basic English prose in writing clear and easily understood reports. Perhaps his most specific statement about style is the following: "It is my contention that any statement found in psychological reports could be made comprehensible to any literate individual of at least average intelligence" (p. 58). By inference, Klopfer believes that reports should be written with a minimum of technical vocabulary and in a manner that places readability ahead of other grammatic concerns.

In another early discussion, Huber (1961) admonishes the writer to develop his or her own style. Huber suggests that "report writing is to some degree an art in the sense that the writer's personality and outlook are imposed on the data. . . . Style of writing is one of the means by which a writer imposes his personality on a report" (p. 81). He goes on to say that "you should resist anyone's imposing a style on you" (p. 81). Huber thus emphasizes the personal nature of the choices the writer must make in developing style and apparently suggests that the writer's own interest in developing a style is the primary method by which a personal style can evolve.

Tallent (1976) identifies three styles of writing in reports: scientific, literary, and journalistic. The scientific style might mimic the objectivity of the write-up of a laboratory experiment and, thereby, imply a degree of scientific accuracy. An example of this style might be: "These test scores and observations confirm the hypothesis that the child is emotionally labile due to the home situation." A literary style might use multiple modifiers, even to the point of exaggeration, with the intention of conveying a vivid picture of the client: "The child's outrageous behavior derives from the appalling home situation and the unfortunate child's enormous difficulty in coping with it." A journalistic style attempts to convey a maximum amount of information succinctly by relying on short sentences and commonplace vocabulary: "The behavior that is giving the teacher trouble is caused by the child's problems at home." Aspects of each of these styles have a place in certain contexts; different situations may merit the erudition of the scientific style, the expressiveness of the literary style, or the bluntness of the journalistic style.

Hollis and Donn (1979) state that, "the best stylistic approach in preparing the psychological report is to endeavor to be clear, simple, concise, orderly and developmental" (p. 122). They go on to list several rules for style and state that the report should clearly reflect the individuality of the client about whom it is written rather than using stereotyped terms or phrases that might be applicable to any number of clients. They argue that conclusions should be advanced "as straightforwardly as the validity and reliability of data and information will permit" (p. 123). Hollis and Donn note that writers should prefer short words, short sentences, and short paragraphs. They suggest that each paragraph should contain just one main thought. Thus, these authors advocate a style that emphasizes simple vocabulary and grammatic constructions.

Blau (1991) also argues for short sentences with one concept in each.

He also recommends short paragraphs and generally stresses brevity: "Conciseness is vital. Few reports are written that could not have been shorter" (p. 198). He is aware of the importance of organizing the report in a narrative fashion: "There should be a logical sequence in the presentation of material. The report should tell a story . . ." (p. 198). Finally, Blau argues explicitly that the report should appeal to the reader, stating "A report should awaken and keep the interest of the reader" (p. 198). Blau thus stresses the importance of writing concisely, organizing the report logically, and making the report interesting to the reader.

Another source on style worth consideration is the *Publication Manual of the American Psychological Association*, which serves as a standard in many areas of psychology. The authors of the *Manual* emphasize the need for orderly presentation of ideas, smoothness of expression, economy of expression, and precision in word choice. They note with respect to sentence length that "although writing only in short, simple sentences produces choppy and boring prose, writing exclusively in long, involved sentences creates difficult, sometimes incomprehensible material. Varied sentence length helps readers maintain interest and comprehension" (1994, p. 28). They make the point about vocabulary and grammatic structure in a way that provides an illustration: "Direct, declarative sentences with simple, common words are usually best" (p. 28). Finally, the authors of the *Manual* suggest that paragraph length also be varied: "Single-sentence paragraphs are abrupt. Paragraphs that are too long are likely to lose the reader's attention. New paragraphs provide a pause for the reader—a chance to assimilate one step in the conceptual development before beginning another" (p. 28). The authors of the *Manual* provide recommendations similar to those of several other authors in suggesting the need for simple and direct communication. They make the additional recommendation, however, that vocabulary and grammatic structure should vary in order to make the writing more interesting to the reader.

The Professional Style

As with other topics in report writing, there is insufficient research about style to make recommendations about language use in reports. Here again, however, a consensus can be drawn from what authorities have written. The style suggested by this consensus can be called the *professional style*. This phrase emphasizes that it is not literary or journalistic, but a style that is appropriate for communicating important information gained from technical procedures. Its elements can be summarized as follows:

1. In the area of *vocabulary choice*, the writer using the professional style will choose words that have these characteristics:
   - common usage (widespread rather than prevalent)
   - shortness (skill rather than competency)
   - inclusion in standard general reference works (not technical vocabulary)
   - precise meaning (have a specific use with a clear significance)
2. In the area of *grammatic structure*, the writer will choose a variety of sentence constructions and lengths as appropriate to the content to help maintain the reader's interest.
3. At the level of *paragraph structure*, the writer will tend to keep paragraphs short and focused on a single concept. Similar but related concepts will be contained in separate paragraphs that are physically close to each other and that are connected by concluding and topic sentences.

There are several advantages to this formulation of style. It is consistent with what virtually every authority on writing in psychology suggests, yet it is flexible enough to give writers freedom to develop a personally effective mode of expression. It is neither overly prescriptive nor so vague as to be useless as a guide for the writer. In addition, it goes beyond exhortations to use simple words and sentences in written communication and recognizes that writers should vary word choice and sentence length in order to avoid monotony. Whether a word or usage satisfies these three criteria can be checked; if the writer is in doubt about whether word choice or grammatic structure is consistent with professional style, he or she can refer to the three elements listed.

In the area of vocabulary, for example, the writer might be unsure whether a word such as *arduous* is appropriate for use in a report to be sent to a social worker in a community agency. Tests suggested above are common usage and shortness.

Therefore, the writer should decide whether there is a more common or shorter word, perhaps by consulting a dictionary of synonyms. Although arduous is a word in standard English, *difficult* is more common and is probably preferable. Similar tests can be devised for determining whether writing is consistent with other elements of professional style.

Some Common Problems

Although an exhaustive catalog of stylistic problems is beyond the scope of this book, some problems are unique to psychological report writing and are discussed here. If you are concerned with stylistic problems in general, you might refer to Strunk and White's (1979) classic *The Elements of Style*. Few short books do a better job of discussing basic principles of writing. The *Publication Manual of the American Psychological Association* (American Psychological Association, 1994) also provides a discussion of specific style problems encountered in psychological writing, although much of it deals with writing about research investigations. What follows, then, is a listing of some common problems specific to report writing with suggested solutions.

Perhaps the most common stylistic problem specific to report writing is the author's failure to keep in mind the difference between the client and the client's test scores. For example:

POOR: The client was in the average range of ability.
BETTER: The client's score fell in the average range.

Here, the writer must keep in mind that test scores describe aspects of the client's functioning, but do not define the person. The same principle holds when discussing a diagnosis:

POOR: The mentally retarded often require close supervision. Psychotics sometimes recover completely.
BETTER: Developmentally disabled persons often require close supervision. Persons with psychotic symptoms sometimes recover completely.
EVEN BETTER: Persons with low levels of general intellectual ability and adaptive behavior deficits often require close supervision. Persons who have difficulties with real-

ity testing and have disabling social skills deficits
sometimes recover completely.

In these examples, the writer can emphasize the important distinction
between a diagnosis and the person being diagnosed. In the example
labeled Even Better, the writer has gone beyond this distinction to
provide concrete examples of the types of problems that impair these
persons' functioning. Although this approach requires more words, it
may have the effect of encouraging the reader to think about the client
as a unique individual with certain problems in living. If these problems in living are addressed specifically in the recommendations, the
reader may be more optimistic about his or her ability to help the client. Sudduth's (1976) study, reviewed in chapter 2, suggests precisely
this.

A common complaint of readers of psychological reports is that
writers hedge their statements with too many modifiers:

> POOR: It appears at least somewhat possible that the client
> may develop a potentially more serious disorder.
>
> BETTER: The client may develop a more serious disorder.

Notice that the second example preserves the author's intent to signal
to the reader that the outcome "develop a more serious disorder" is
only a possibility—but one that merits concern. A similar problem
occurs in reporting test scores:

> POOR: These test results suggest the possibility that the cli-
> ent may be only mildly disabled.
>
> BETTER: These test results show that the client may be only
> mildly disabled.

Again, the second sentence preserves a degree of doubt appropriate
when results do not allow greater certainty.

Another problem in this area is the need for writers to qualify statements judiciously with words such as *suggest, may indicate,* or *may show*
when assessment data cannot be interpreted validly with more confidence. The writer should keep in mind that the relationship between
any psychological test score and the client's later behavior is only a
probability. Although there may be a great likelihood that a person with
certain test scores will display particular behaviors, the writer should
qualify predictions about the client's current and future function when

predicted behaviors have not been observed directly. On the other hand, when the author has observed behaviors or obtained test scores directly, the more vigorous active voice should be used. The following examples show this distinction, with the verbs and qualifiers in italics:

> Results of this assessment *indicate* that the client *continues to show* a number of behaviors and thought processes characteristic of schizophrenia. Results thus *suggest* that although at present she is functioning well, ongoing monitoring by mental health professionals *may be required* for her to continue to function at this level.

Here, the writer makes clear the difference between facts known with reasonable certainty (behaviors and thought processes) and predictions based only on probabilities, by appropriate qualification of the words used to discuss the client. This practice should be differentiated from the inappropriate hedging illustrated above.

Here is an example that deals with reporting test results:

> Ability testing *indicates* that Martha is *probably functioning* in the low average range of general intellectual ability.

Some authors might quarrel with the word *probably* in this sentence and might suggest that the test result shows conclusively that Martha's intellectual functioning is in the low average range. However, this interpretation of test scores is purposely imprecise because many factors could have intervened to prevent Martha from scoring higher. If the author of this report were required to testify about the assessment in court, for example, the statement "probably functioning" would be defensible under cross-examination because the psychologist has only stated that the test score may indicate something about the client. A statement made with absolute certainty would be difficult to defend.

Once he or she appreciates this distinction, the writer should strive to make it equally clear to the reader. If there is uncertainty in an observation, the writer should not be subtle in communicating this fact to the reader. If reasonable certainty exists about a statement, a direct statement should be made. At times, additional information can help to clarify this issue, as in the following example:

> POOR: The client appeared nervous during test administration.

BETTER: The client's behavior, such as nervous smiles, trembling hands, and a tentative approach to tasks, suggests that he was nervous during assessment.

You may notice that the second statement conforms to the guidelines of the model, while the first does not. The model helps you to be more specific.

One final stylistic issue: It is essential that the author of a report, no less than authors in other contexts in psychology, avoid the use of language or expressions that indicate ethnic or gender stereotyping. These issues are discussed at length in the *Publication Manual* (American Psychological Association, 1994, pp. 46–60); if you are unsure of the appropriate way to express what you wish to say, consult the *Manual.*

The purpose of this discussion of style is to help you learn ways to communicate the results of your assessments more effectively. Beyond these general guidelines about vocabulary and structure, you may wish to consult one of the style manuals suggested above. A final comment on style, provided by Taylor and Teicher (1946), is still relevant today:

The writer need not be overly concerned with making . . . [the] report "professional." A studied attempt at being "professional" or at being "scientific" not only robs the psychological reporting of the dynamic qualities which distinguish a human relationship from an experiment with test tubes, but, more seriously, invariably reflects a basic attitude in the psychologist which will prevent . . . [him or her] from establishing a warm, genuine, friendly rapport. (p. 332)

Improving Writing Style

You can work to improve your style by doing several things when you write. Using the materials in Appendices A, B, and C will help you learn how to use the expository process model and diagnose problems in the reports you already write. Using the model, perhaps by filling out the worksheets provided in chapter 4, will help you create a more concise and logical organization for the report you write; in addition, the report will be based in the raw data of the assessment. If you follow the guidelines provided above on vocabulary choice and grammatic structure, you should be able to write reports in manageable sections that encourage the reader to find out what is contained in them rather than overwhelming the reader with page-length paragraphs.

The *Publication Manual of the American Psychological Association* (American Psychological Association, 1994) also includes suggestions for improving your writing (p. 31). The authors of the *Manual* suggest that you write from an outline, put a draft aside and return to it after a day or two, and then ask a colleague to read it and give you feedback about it. These are all excellent ways to obtain a fresh perspective on your writing, for when you work on something intently it is easy to become so immersed in it that you lose your objectivity. Things that are obviously unclear or awkward on a rereading may have seemed completely correct earlier. Working from an outline seems to require additional effort, but, in fact, it can ultimately reduce the work by streamlining the process of writing the final draft. Organizing your thoughts by means of an outline is one way to make sure that you know what you want to write, and when you know what you want to write, you are far less likely to become entangled in a stylistic morass later on; as Woodford (1967) has suggested, there may be a close relationship between clear writing and clear thinking.

You also should recognize that economical and clear expression in report writing is not a goal that, once attained, can be ignored in favor of more interesting pursuits. Learning to write well must be a continuing process in which you obtain feedback about your writing and modify it on the basis of the information received. Feedback can be of the formal type suggested by Ownby and Wallbrown (1983), or you can give yourself feedback by rereading reports after an interval or by asking colleagues for feedback about what you have written. More suggestions for improving your reports are contained in Appendix B. These are valuable ways of developing a more readable and effective style.

Summary

This chapter has reviewed common problems in choice of report model and linguistic style. Problems with the report model usually stem from a failure to consider the purpose of the report and the needs of the reader. Several models were reviewed, and suggestions for the use of each were made. Only a few specific recommendations about style were presented. In general, the specifics of style have been left to the writer to learn for him- or herself because learning style is, in part, the same as learning to write—and this book cannot serve that function. Style cannot be learned in a mechanical way, though devices such as the expository process model can help. Style must be developed through the interaction of writer preferences and the demands of the assessment task. For these reasons, you are encouraged to use the techniques suggested for improving your writing and to consult an authoritative reference whenever necessary. In this way, your style can become better in the specific instance and can develop over a period of time into a more effective tool for communication.

6

THE REPORT IN CONTEXT

This chapter discusses how to tailor your report so that it will be effective in the context in which it is used. The need for writing reports that are individualized with respect to the client and his or her situation has already been stressed; this chapter covers specifics about how to do this. It presents a way to think about report contexts and to assess them according to their complexity. Ways to modify your writing based on your assessment of the report's context are also suggested. Before considering the context of the report in detail, however, you should consider how to develop the overall concept of the report.

Developing the Overall Concept

The importance of developing an overall concept for a report is emphasized by several authorities, including Klopfer (1960) and Huber (1961). Klopfer, for example, suggests that lack of focus is a common problem:

> Inexperienced and poorly trained psychologists have a tendency to put together an indigestible mass of discreet observations and a 'cook book' list of signs and indicators without any sort of overview or attempt to apply these to the problems which prompted the original referral (p.7).

Huber, like Klopfer, devotes an entire chapter to the topic. Hollis and Donn (1979, p. 20) concur that lack of focus is a problem in report writing.

If the consensus of authorities is that the writer should establish an overall concept or formulation for the assessment report, how, you might legitimately ask, is this task to be carried out? The simplest and probably the best way of developing an overall concept for the report is to clearly define the questions addressed by the assessment and respond to them briefly. If you are writing a hypothesis-oriented report, a statement of the answers to the assessment questions can serve as the first paragraph of the Assessment Results section, while if you are writing a domain-oriented report, the answers can be supplied in the sections where they are most relevant to the data.

Take the case of Mr. Fiduciary, a 45-year-old man who was referred by his physician because he complains of being constantly tired (without physical basis) and of lacking the energy to work in his successful accounting business. Test results show high scores on scale 2 of the MMPI (this probably indicates depression); an interview with the man reveals that he has lost about 15 pounds during the last 3 months and that he often wakes up early in the morning and can't get back to sleep. The man does not complain of low mood, but the interview also reveals that he and his wife were divorced about 6 months ago and that he has distant relationships with his children and other family members. He lives alone. Thus, the assessment data clearly suggest that the man is depressed (the middle-level construct in the expository process model worksheet illustrated in the lower portion of Figure 6.1). Assessment data are referenced to this construct, the only one that will be discussed at present.

The referral problem in the top portion of Figure 6.1 is listed in the Problems and Questions section as the referring physician might have stated it, although perhaps the psychologist will have made it more direct and rendered it as a question: "What is the reason for Mr. Fiduciary's lack of energy?" In addition, the implicit question "What can be done about it?" is added because it is likely that the physician will want an opinion about what should be done to help Mr. Fiduciary, even if the physician does not say so explicitly. The answers to the problem are listed in the Answers section: "The client is depressed," "Attempt to involve the client in therapy," and "Suggest a trial of antidepressant medication" (if you know the physician will welcome advice on this sort of issue).

Questions		Answers	
1.	What is the reason for Mr. Fiduciary's lack of energy?	1.	He is depressed
2.	What can be done about it?	2.a.	Provide psychotherapy
		2.b.	Try antidepressant medication

MR. FIDUCIARY'S EPM WORKSHEET

Data	MLC	Conclusion	Recommendation
Complains he is tired			Provide psychotherapy
Has lost weight		Depression is present	
Sleep disturbance			Try antidepressants

Figure 6.1   Assessment Questions and Answers

When you are writing the actual report, then, you might draw the Reason for Referral section directly from the form and say something such as, "Mr. Fiduciary was referred by his physician, Dr. B. Pressure, for evaluation of his difficulties with constant feelings of tiredness that have interfered with his ability to work." The Background Information section of the report can be written from the personal history data listed on the expository process model worksheet. It's important to write this section from the model worksheet rather than from notes because writing from the model worksheet ensures that all of the interview data you include will be related to the central focus of the report. If you write from your notes, you may include interesting bits of information about the client that are unrelated to the assessment questions.

If you write a hypothesis-oriented report, as might be appropriate when responding to a specific question posed by a physician, you could write the first paragraph of the Assessment Results section from the Answers section of the form. In the case of Mr. Fiduciary, this might be a brief paragraph:

> Results of this assessment suggest that the reason for Mr. Fiduciary's persistent feelings of tiredness and difficulties in working is that he is depressed. Test results and information obtained on interview support this idea; interview data also indicate possible reasons why Mr. Fiduciary may be depressed.

This paragraph could be followed by a series of paragraphs, each of which deals with a separate issue, such as evidence for Mr. Fiduciary being depressed, the life events that may have caused his depression, and how Mr. Fiduciary views his current life situation.

In this way, the two forms, Assessment Questions and Answers (top of Figure 6.1) and the Expository Process Model Worksheet (Figure 4.6 and bottom of Figure 6.1), provide structure that allows you to develop an overall concept of the assessment. With this concept, writing the rest of the report will be much easier, and it is almost certain that you will not simply give the reader "an indigestible mass of discreet observations" (Klopfer, 1960, p. 7). Practice in using the two forms will allow you to develop the skill of determining the overall concept of the report. Once it is conceptualized, you must consider how the report is to function in its context.

Assessment of Context

Nearly all authorities on report writing emphasize the importance of tailoring the report to its context. This process requires that you use writing style and report format and model to create a report that will be useful to your reader. Changes in style, for example, will not be limited to using specific words but will also include how you choose vocabulary and grammatic structure. These changes should take into account the report's intended reader, the assessment problem, and the environment. Each of these is a dimension of the report's context and can be individually assessed.

Assessing the Referral Agent

This context dimension can be assessed on the following factors: (a) professional affiliation of the referral source, (b) level of professional training, and (c) complexity of the referral source. The meanings of the first two factors are probably clear; the third deals with the occasionally ambiguous motivations of the referral agent as he or she functions in the broader context of an institution such as a hospital, school, or community agency.

Considering the professional identity of the referral source is important. Reports written for a physician, attorney, psychologist, teacher, or social worker may differ in format, model, or style. The report to a physician about a specific question, for example, might be a short letter based on the hypothesis-oriented model. It might give a summary of the assessment and its implications for client treatment. The report to a special education teacher about the same assessment might be a longer, domain-oriented report. (See also chapter 7.)

Here is an example of two reports written about the same child, referred for evaluation because of an unusually high activity level and problems paying attention in class. The first report is to the pediatric neurologist who referred the child for evaluation. The neurologist knows the psychologist both personally and professionally, an aspect of the situation that affects the tone of the language (it is more informal for a person known to the psychologist), the amount of raw data included in the report (the neurologist knows and trusts the psychologist's statements on the basis of past experience), and even the closing used in the letter—"cordially" rather than "sincerely."

Dear Dr. Neuro,

I saw your patient, Billy Active (DOB: 10-8-88), on your referral for evaluation of his difficulties with a high activity level and problems paying attention in class. Results of my assessment show that Billy probably displays an unusually high activity level (suggested both by his teacher's responses to the Conners Rating Scale and my observations of him in the office) and significant problems in attending in the large group situation.

Billy's scores on subtests of the WISC-III that require attention were particularly low (for example, Digit Span subtest scaled score = 4, or the 2nd percentile; Coding subtest scaled score = 5, or the 5th percentile). These scores are in contrast to Billy's performances on both verbal and nonverbal subtests, which were uniformly in the high average to superior range (for example, Vocabulary scaled score = 15, or the 95th percentile).

Overall, these results suggest that Billy presents a clear case of Attention-Deficit/Hyperactivity Disorder and they would certainly support a trial of stimulant medication to determine whether it can be helpful in managing Billy's difficulties. I would recommend that Billy be reassessed in 9 months to a year in order to monitor his progress in acquiring academic skills and that his response to medication, if you elect to try this route, be monitored by his teacher through the ongoing use of a rating scale such as the Conners.

> Cordially,
> Childe Psychologist

The following is an excerpt from a more lengthy report supplied to the special education teacher working with Billy. He or she is more likely to be interested in details of the behavioral assessment and in suggestions for instructional and behavioral management of the child in both large class and small group settings:

PSYCHOLOGICAL REPORT

Name: Billy Active   *DOB*: 10-8-88
Address: Suburbantown, State   *Date seen*: 1-5-96
Psychologist: C. Psychologist, Ph.D

Reason for Referral

Billy was referred for evaluation by Dr. Neuro, his pediatric neurologist. Dr. Neuro requested evaluation of Billy's high level of activity and his reported difficulties paying attention in the classroom.

Background Information

[This section would include relevant medical and personal history data about Billy. It might also include results of previous psychological and speech pathology evaluations carried out by the school and other agencies.]

Assessment Results

SOURCES OF INFORMATION
Wechsler Intelligence Scale for Children–3rd edition (WISC-III)
Woodcock-Johnson Psycho-Educational Battery (WJPEB)

. . .

[Other assessment measures would be listed here.] Conners Pupil Rating Scale (Conners) completed by Ms. Landsdowne, Billy's regular classroom teacher.

Results of this assessment show that Billy is probably functioning in the high average range of general intellectual ability (WISC-III Verbal IQ = 118; Performance IQ = 109; Full Scale IQ = 114). Billy's scores on subtests of the WISC-III that require attention and sustained concentration, however, were much lower than these overall indices of his intellectual functioning. For example, on a measure of his ability to remember sequences of orally presented digits, his score was at the 2nd percentile (Digit Span subtest), while his score on a measure of rapid manipulation of symbols—entering small geometric symbols according to a numbered key—was at the 5th percentile (Coding subtest). Children who score at these levels on these subtests are often described as having difficulties in sustaining attention in the large classroom environment and are seen by others as having a short attention span and possible problems in learning.

. . .

[Other assessment results might be explained here.]

Assessment of Billy's reading skills suggests that although his reading achievement overall is not significantly below that expected for his age or estimated ability (WJPEB standard score for reading cluster = 108), he may have developed some poor strategies in reading that could be addressed in reading instruction. For example, on a sight word recognition task, Billy tended to rely on an impulsive strategy in which he only scanned the initial and final consonants before responding. Thus, he might easily confuse the words *cat* and *cut* because they differ only in their medial vowels. . . . [Additional data about Billy's reading skills would be discussed here.]

Assessment of Billy's behavioral functioning through behavioral rating scale (Conners), observation, and parent and teacher report suggests that his general activity level is far higher than that of most children his age. It may also be noted that Billy's behavior is usually not well-directed or organized and can at times become frustrating to him as well as to those around him. . . . [Additional information about Billy's behavior might be inserted here.]

. . .

[Additional assessment information might be reported here.]

Summary and Recommendations

Results of this assessment show that Billy probably displays an unusually high level of activity along with educationally important difficulties in sustaining attention. It can also be noted that these difficulties are probably more severe in the large classroom setting than in small group tutoring or one-to-one testing situations. . . .

The following recommendations may be useful to those working with Billy:

1. It probably would be helpful for those who are working with Billy to arrange a cueing system with him to help remind him to pay attention in class. A nonverbal cue, such as a hand sign, might be an effective cue for Billy and at the same time would minimize the potentially negative effects of giving him attention for problematic behavior. Giving him attention for his nonattending behavior might have the effect of making it more likely to occur.

2. In reading work with Billy, it might be useful to encourage him to adopt a more reflective strategy in word recognition tasks, both in isolation and in context. He might be encouraged to say something such as "stop and think" to himself before he responds about a word. It might also be useful to encourage Billy directly to scan the middle of words before responding because it is with this aspect of word recognition skills that he has the most obvious difficulties.

3. Medical evaluation for possible use of stimulant medication as part of a coordinated plan of behavioral and educational interventions for dealing with Billy's high activity level is indicated.

Although the second report is schematic, it is quickly apparent that it contains substantially more specific information about the child in question. The physician is primarily interested in knowing whether the psychologist thinks Billy is hyperactive and what the educational and medical implications of the problem may be. Depending on the physician, he or she may be interested in a statement of the potential usefulness of medication, although such a recommendation should be included only when the psychologist is certain that it will be welcomed—physicians vary widely in their interest in suggestions from other health care professionals. In this case, Dr. Psychologist knew Dr. Neuro and was able to treat the subject of Billy's behavior briefly and informally.

By contrast, Dr. Psychologist's report for the school is more detailed in providing specifics of test data, in which the teacher is likely to have an interest, as well as in detailing how the test and observational data relate to Billy's school behavior. The formal Recommendations section provides specific techniques that the teacher could implement in large and small group settings for dealing with Billy's attention and behavior problems. Note that Billy's impulsivity already intrudes into his reading skills and that Dr. Psychologist includes suggestions for preventing Billy from becoming worse in this area.

Level of training. The question of style with various referral sources is less clear, but can be addressed on the basis of level of professional training. The style of a report written about a client who is schizophrenic for a physician with specialized training in psychiatry, for example, will be quite different from that of a similar report written for a social worker in a public welfare agency. This is true because the two readers probably vary widely in the amount of background information they possess and their needs for information about the client are different. The psychiatrist may be interested in detailed and technical information about the client's mental status as he or she adjusts the client's medication for optimal effect, while the social worker may be most interested in a general statement about the client's functioning that will be helpful in establishing the client's disability for the purpose of obtaining financial support from government sources. Here, you can see that level of training and profession interact; the psychiatrist will probably receive the more detailed and more technical report, and the social worker will receive the less detailed and less technical report.

Complexity. Assessing the complexity of the referral source requires both diplomacy and insight. At the outset, it should be acknowledged that the referrer's own needs and feelings, as well as the interests of the client referred, enter into the decision to make a referral for evaluation. The situations that are the most difficult for the psychologist to influence are often those in which the motivations of the referral agent are complex and impinge on the client's situation. Successful completion of the report requires as clear an understanding as possible of why the referral was made. The dimensions by which the referring agent can be assessed in this area are the complexity and openness of the agent's agenda in referring the client for evaluation. An example of a simple and open agenda might be when a client in a medical hospital is referred for evaluation prior to some form of treatment. The referring agent, usually a physician, will want baseline information about the client's cognitive and emotional functioning prior to initiating treatment, such as radiation for treatment of cancer, in order to evaluate its possible effects. A complex and hidden agenda referral might occur in a community agency when a staff therapist and his or her supervisor disagree on an appropriate course of action for a client. The therapist might refer the client for evaluation in the hope that the psychologist's opinion will bolster the therapist's point of view. Here, the psychologist risks becoming ensnared in a disagreement between two other parties. The psychologist can play a useful role in such a situation, but risks alienating one or both parties in the struggle if the report doesn't address the referral questions diplomatically.

There is perhaps some irony in the fact that assessment of this aspect of the referral process may be at once the least directly related to the client's needs and the most important in the psychologist's professional success in establishing an influential relationship with the referral agent. This is a critical step in helping the agent modify his or her approach to working with the client. The psychologist's success in this effort greatly affects how his or her recommendations are viewed and the degree to which they are implemented. To complicate the problem further, the referral agent may not even be aware of, or at least not be willing to acknowledge, his or her motivations.

Hidden agendas. The referral agent's motivations in making a referral can be understood as consisting of open, or acknowledged, and hidden, or unacknowledged, agendas. The referral agent's open agenda includes whatever public statement he or she makes about the reason for the referral, such as a request for guidance in planning treatment for a client, in helping a child learn to read, or in determining the fitness of a potential employee for a position. The agent's referral request might also be accompanied by requests for additional information, such as a general description of the client's personality, information about behavioral management strategies likely to be useful with a child, or the potential employee's likelihood of success in a higher-level position. Most referrals come to the psychologist with this sort of open agenda, prompted by the referral agent's sincere desire to help the client function well.

For various reasons, however, the referral agent's agenda may be partially hidden. One case in which a referral source may not openly acknowledge his or her interests when making the referral is when he or she is aware that the psychologist's help may be useful, but perceives that accepting the help is an indication of personal failure in working with a client. Such persons may request the psychologist's assistance, but then be reluctant to try any of the recommendations developed from the assessment results. In addition, interventions that the agent may be persuaded to try often fail in this situation, perhaps because of the agent's limited motivation to make them work. In extreme cases, the agent may simultaneously acknowledge that an evaluation was requested, but deny the need for help subsequent to the evaluation, even in the face of objective indications that such help is needed.

Another case in which the referral agent might have a partially hidden agenda arises in school psychology settings in which a teacher is discouraged about his or her ability to deal with a child and wants the child placed in a special education classroom. The teacher ostensibly may ask the psychologist for assistance in helping the child to function in the educational environment, but in reality the teacher wants the psychologist's test data to help justify the removal of the child from the classroom. Here, the school psychologist's task is formidable in using both report and consultation to persuade the teacher to try new ways of helping the child.

Yet another problem that involves both open and hidden agendas, already alluded to above, is when two persons disagree on the nature of the client's problem or the steps required to deal with it. In this instance, the psychologist may be asked to evaluate in the hope that the psychologist's data will support one side of an argument that, at times, can be unrelated to a determination of the client's welfare. It is not always possible for the consulting psychologist to be aware that this sort of situation exists. When unsure, the psychologist can often be of greatest service to the client by providing an honest opinion on the best course of action for the client, even when this opinion may run counter to that of other persons who are working with the client. Regardless of the political involvements, the psychologist's first duty is always to the welfare of the client. The psychologist cannot allow external circumstances to influence his or her report on a client until this obligation is fulfilled (albeit as tactfully as possible).

Assessing the Referral Problem

Many reports are unsatisfactory because the psychologist does not adequately determine the nature of the referral problem prior to writing. It is not possible to write a report of a problem-oriented assessment if the problem and its relationship to the environment variables are not specified clearly. A learning problem, for example, might be a teacher's primary concern in referring a child, but the alert psychologist will assess the child's behavior in other contexts as well, and will look for clues about how the child's behavior may be related to the observed learning problem.

One way of making a more detailed assessment of the problem is to arrange a formal or informal conference with the referral agent prior to initiating assessment activities. This sort of assessment might be formal in situations in which the psychologist needs additional information or feels it is to his or her advantage to explore the referral agent's concerns about the client at length. The conference can be as informal as a telephone conversation in which the psychologist briefly discusses the client's problems with the referral agent in order to ascertain precisely what sort of information the agent wants about the client. As a result of this conference, the psychologist should be able to make a succinct statement of the referral problems, often in the form of a series of questions.

Here is an example of how the reason for referral can be clarified by means of a brief conference. The following was written on a referral form sent to a psychologist in a community mental health agency: "<u>Reason for Referral</u>: I'm referring the client for evaluation to find out information to help in therapeutic planning." This reason for referral is vague. Although the psychologist might have chosen to write a general-description type of report in the hope that the information contained might be helpful to the referral agent, in this instance the psychologist telephoned the agent. The psychologist thanked the agent for the referral and asked whether there were any specific questions to be addressed in the evaluation report. The agent responded that her central concern was in finding out whether the child's abusive family background had significantly affected the child's emotional functioning and, if so, in what way. This brief telephone contact resulted in an important clarification of the referral problem; the referral agent had not wanted to write such sensitive information on the referral form and had not had the time to contact the psychologist directly.

Another way in which the referral problem can be clarified further for purposes of assessment is to use the Referral Problems Category System, either adult or child version. The categories within these two systems have proven useful in describing both child and adult referral problems in school, hospital, and community mental health center settings (Ownby, 1986b; Ownby et al., 1984; Ownby et al., 1985; Westman, Ownby, & Smith, 1987). Use of this system allows the report writer to determine what sort of report is likely to be most effective by context and by professional to whom the report is transmitted. For example, a referral might be received from a psychiatrist requesting evaluation of a client's overall mental status. The referral problems category system (Ownby, 1986b) suggests that for a general-understanding type of referral by a physician, the format of the report should be a letter (see chapter 7 for further explanation); the model of the report should be modified hypothesis-oriented, or question-oriented; and the style should be formal professional. When the referring agent is a teacher in the public school who is asking for a general understanding of a child in his or her classroom, the category system suggests that the format of the report should be standard narrative, the model of the report should be domain-oriented, and the style should be formal professional. Although the detailed explanation of assessment findings depends on the assessment results themselves, some of the reporting variables can be determined by the nature of the referral problem and the referral agent.

Assessing the Referral Environment

Assessment of the environment into which the report is to be sent includes consideration of the setting in which its primary intended reader functions (for example, clinic, hospital, school, or agency); whether that setting implies that the report must be written for both primary and secondary readers (as might be true in a school setting, in which the teacher, counselor, and administrator might all read the report); and which of the several discrete functions of the report (such as communicating or providing a record of the assessment) are most important within the assessment context.

The complexity of the setting can be determined easily from knowledge of the referral agent. Settings can be rated as high, medium, or low complexity depending on the number of likely readers of various professional backgrounds by whom the report is likely to be seen. A low complexity setting might be a report sent to a physician in private practice. In this case, there is only a primary reader (the physician); because there are no secondary readers, the characteristics of varying professional backgrounds need not be considered. A high complexity setting would be a psychiatric or rehabilitation hospital that utilizes a team approach. In this case, there will probably be one primary reader and a number of secondary readers. A large number of professional disciplines will probably be represented, including medicine, nursing, occupational and physical therapy, speech pathology, and other programming specialties. The complexity of the setting will affect the way the psychologist writes the report through his or her use of language, middle-level constructs, style, and organization.

Here are complexity estimates for a number of typical settings in which psychologists might write reports:

Psychiatric Inpatient: high complexity because of the large number of secondary readers and the diversity of professional backgrounds represented. The psychologist must be concerned with both primary and secondary readers' knowledge of assessment procedures and the middle-level constructs used in reports.

Community Mental Health Center: high complexity, again because of the large number of secondary readers and the diversity of their backgrounds.

School Setting: moderate complexity. The report is likely to be used by the primary reader, usually the classroom teacher, and perhaps also by the counselor, administrator, or special education specialist. Even though there are a fairly large number of potential secondary readers, their professional backgrounds are similar.

Industrial Setting: moderate complexity. In the industrial setting, the report is likely to be read both by primary readers, such as the personnel manager or assistants, and by secondary readers in management positions. As in the school setting, although there are a large number of potential secondary readers, their professional backgrounds are similar.

Private Practice Psychologist: low complexity. Even though the report might be read by several persons in a group practice, the characteristics of the primary and secondary readers will be similar, which will allow the writer to make an estimate of the readers' characteristics.

Private Practice Physician: low complexity. There probably will be one primary reader and no secondary reader. The writer will be able to make an accurate estimate of the characteristics of the report's reader.

Tailoring Message Discrepancy

The overall purpose of the report has been defined as providing credible and persuasive statements to the report's readers. Consistent with the professional nature of psychological reports, the primary emphasis of this book has been on ways to make statements credible to readers with the explicit assumption that credible statements are most likely to be persuasive as well. This section, however, will consider in detail ways to make statements more persuasive to more readers. Research on the social psychology of persuasive communication (McGuire, 1985; Tedeschi & Lindskold, 1976, pp. 321–364) and the social influence theory of counseling (Strong, 1968) will be discussed.

Research in social psychology that deals with persuasive communication has focused heavily on the discrepancy of the message's content with the receiver's own belief system. In general, research has shown that messages that are moderately discrepant from the receiver's beliefs are likely to produce the largest amount of attitude change in the receiver, although a number of factors may affect this outcome. Petty and Cacioppo (1986), for example, argue that an issue of central importance in attitude change regardless of discrepancy is the extent to which the persuasive message is processed by its receiver. Several things, such as format, attractiveness, and salience, can influence extent of message processing and, thereby, affect the persuasiveness of the communication. The implications of their model for reports are clear. The psychologist should strive to ensure the greatest degree of processing of the message because this is likely to produce the greatest attitude change (assuming that the message is correct, well reasoned, and well presented). Therefore, the report should be visually appealing, well organized with headings and subheadings, and succinct.

Beyond the issues of trying to guarantee that the report is read completely and its message extensively processed, it is clear that the message should be presented tactfully to make it more acceptable to the reader. The report's message should not be widely discrepant from the beliefs of the primary (and possibly secondary) reader in order for it to produce the largest attitude change. If, for example, the referring physician is confident that a client is not in fact experiencing anxiety, but merely complaining of anxiety in order to gain attention, it may be most effective not to make a strong statement in the report that the client is extremely anxious. Instead, you can make a statement that various test indices show that anxiety may be present and perhaps include a discussion of the alternative hypothesis that the client is merely complaining of anxiety. By considering both possibilities, the conclusions in your report will not appear as discrepant from the referral agent's own beliefs, and he or she will not be as likely to discount them.

Another example might arise in the instance of a classroom teacher who insists that a child is completely capable of learning, but for some unknown reason has chosen not to do so—often, this child is termed lazy. Your testing, by contrast, might indicate that the child is suffering from a learning disorder of sufficient magnitude to impair the child's functioning. Here, you might tailor the message's discrepancy by reviewing the test data that show evidence of a learning disorder and by providing an extensive discussion of the effects of the probable learning disorder on the child's motivational status. In this way, the message is congruent with the beliefs of the reader with respect to observations of the child's motivational status, but discrepant with respect to etiology of motivation.

This discussion raises an important ethical problem—the extent to which the reporting of data can be tailored before the psychologist may be guilty of misrepresenting, rather than appropriately communicating, the results of the assessment. Although this is a matter of professional judgment, the examples above illustrate that tailoring the discrepancy of the message may be accomplished not so much by altering the presentation of the data themselves as by altering the context of their interpretation. This approach is consistent with another area of research on persuasive communication, which deals with the results of including a discussion of opposing viewpoints in a persuasive message.

Investigators have shown that the impact of the message may be affected by inclusion of opposing viewpoints, depending on the intelligence of the person who is receiving the message and on the likelihood that the receiver will encounter the opposing viewpoint anyway.

Here, the maximum effect of including a discussion of an opposing viewpoint in a persuasive communication was shown to result when the reader was intelligent and likely to be aware of counterarguments.

As the writer of a psychological report, you can assume that most of your readers are both intelligent and likely to be aware of counterarguments—especially when they themselves have advanced these arguments. Written in professional style, a discussion of possible opposing viewpoints will probably sound well reasoned and professional to your readers. Thus, it is important to consider opposing viewpoints in your report writing, and this may be especially useful as a way of tailoring the discrepancy of the message to your reader's own beliefs.

Social Influence Research

A second area of relevant research is Strong's (1968) analysis of counseling as a social influence process. The close relationship of counseling as an influence process to consultation as an influence process may be apparent; others have referred to consultative influence as stemming from expert and referent sources. It seems likely that similar processes are involved in persuasion in report writing. Strong suggests that the elements of interpersonal influence include expertness, attractiveness, and trustworthiness. Applied to the psychological report, this analysis provides guidance in making reports more influential. In the following discussion, expertness refers to the reader's perception of the writer's expertness and trustworthiness; attractiveness will be considered both as the reader's perception of the writer's attractiveness and the physical attractiveness of the report, which can be viewed as the writer's representative.

In the area of *expertness*, the writer must find ways of communicating to the report's reader that he or she is a highly trained specialist in psychological assessment whose conclusions are based on extensive training and experience. You should not set out to prove your expertness by loading the report with professional jargon—as noted earlier, this approach will be counterproductive. Expertness can be communicated to the reader by writing model-based statements in professional style. Such statements will communicate to readers that you have considered test data carefully and that you are willing to communicate your interpretations in a way that shows the reader your reasoning. This degree of openness reinforces readers' perceptions of your expertness because you are sufficiently confident of your reasoning to subject it to external scrutiny. Tailoring the discrepancy of your message appropriately to the report's intended reader is also likely to enhance the reader's view of your expertness because perceived similarity is an important aspect of positive evaluations of psychologist expertise.

Many studies have shown that perceived *attractiveness* depends on perception of similarity between the target and the perceiver. In report writing, this finding indicates that you should write the report so as to suggest that you are similar to the reader. This can be accomplished by writing in a way that utilizes the other person's constructs or, whenever possible, by emphasizing the similarity of your views of the client's functioning with those of the primary reader. If a child's teacher has observed that the child behaves quite differently toward teachers who are women as opposed to those who are men, you could include a statement such as "Assessment results are consistent with Ms. Brainstorm's observation that Peter is much more likely to disobey directives from male rather than female teachers." In this way, you have emphasized the similarity of your view of the problem with that of the agent, as well as implicitly making a positive statement about the teacher's judgment.

Sorrentino (1985) argues for the importance of considering the visual aspects of presentations of professional writing; the importance of keeping paragraphs short was discussed in chapter 5. Strunk and White (1979) also stress the importance of making what is presented attractive to the reader: "In general, remember that paragraphing calls for a good eye as well as a logical mind. Enormous blocks of print look formidable to a reader. [The reader] has a certain reluctance to tackle them; [he or she] can lose [his or her] way in them" (1979, p. 17). These sentiments are echoed by Hollis and Donn, who recommend that the visual qualities of the report be considered when preparing it: "Typically, a reader's overall perception and evaluation will be adversely affected by the appearance of a report. Not only must the cover have eye appeal but each page and section must entice the reader's visual sense" (1979, p. 128). Blau (1991) also stresses the importance of making the report visually attractive to readers. These authors suggest using white space, varying type size for emphasis, and highlighting key words or ideas as ways of making the report visually appealing. Other considerations in making the report physically attractive include the use of headings to break up the possibly monotonous presentation, the use of an attractive typeface, and being sure that the quality of the typing doesn't affect the reader's perceptions.

Strong's (1968) social influence theory states that perceived counselor *trustworthiness* depends on communication of a sincere interest in the client's problems, a positive attitude toward the client's potential to be helped, and an emphatic statement about the confidentiality of the client's communications; a counselor who communicates interest in the client for personal reasons, such as curiosity, will not be perceived as trustworthy.

You can apply these suggestions to report writing by ensuring that your reports deal with the client's problems in a professional manner that clearly communicates your interest in helping the primary reader to deal with them. Including a balanced description of the client's strengths and weaknesses and specific suggestions for working with the client, as discussed above, may communicate a positive attitude about the client. Communications about the confidentiality of the assessment can be made in several ways. Although some writers place a statement that the report is confidential at the top of the report, it is not clear whether the benefits of this practice outweigh its distracting quality. It may not be necessary to communicate explicitly about the confidentiality of assessment data when the report is transmitted within an agency. Your concern for the confidentiality of the assessment results can be communicated to a reader who is receiving the report outside of an agency by enclosing a copy of the client's signed consent to release information form with a cover letter to the reader to remind him or her that only the psychologist can release the assessment data to another party.

Although these practices may be useful, when you are transmitting assessment information, be alert to the possibility that reminders of the confidentiality of the report may appear overwrought or condescending to other professionals. You can communicate to the reader that you are not interested in the client for inappropriate personal reasons by confining the content of the report to the assessment data, their interpretation, conclusions, and recommendations. If you confine the content of the report to the elements in the expository process model and the referral questions worksheets, it is unlikely that you will appear to be inappropriately interested in other aspects of the client's functioning.

Summary

This chapter has reviewed the assessment of the context of the report and ways to tailor the report so as to produce maximum attitude and behavior change on the part of the reader. Assessing the nature of the problem, the agent, and the environment are all important in considering how the report should be written. The referral problems category system provides a structure for considering how the nature of the problem will affect the model, format, and content of the report. Determining the referral agent's type of professional affiliation, level of professional training, and openness of agenda provides information that will affect the model, format, language, and content of the report. The nature of the environment, and especially the characteristics of the primary reader (the referral agent) and potential secondary readers will also affect the report's language and content. Content suitable to a report written only for another psychologist, for example, might not be suitable for a report written to a psychologist as the primary reader, but whose secondary readers might include professionals in other disciplines.

The final section of the chapter reviewed briefly the way that social psychological research on persuasive communications and social influence can help you write the most effective report. Research suggests that the most effective report will communicate a moderately discrepant message that takes into account opposing viewpoints and that communicates the writer's expertness and trustworthiness in a format that is visually attractive to the reader.

7

ORGANIZATION AND CONTENT OF THE REPORT

How the report is organized into sections and what each section should contain are the topics of this chapter. Ways of organizing reports are called *formats*, and include the business letter, the brief narrative, and the lengthy narrative. Each format is appropriate to certain situations. The report's content also depends on contextual variables, as discussed in chapter 6.

Before turning to specific recommendations, it is helpful to review authorities' suggestions about report formats. A consensus on this topic is easy to find: Almost everyone recommends that the report should be organized in sections such as Reason for Referral, Assessment Results, and so on. Authorities also agree that the report should explain the assessment in a coherent narrative. The report should relate assessment data such as test scores to other pertinent issues, such as the client's age or life situation.

For example, Klopfer (1960) suggests that reports should include Reason for Referral, General Observations, Test Interpretation, and Summary sections. Both Huber (1961) and Tallent (1976) have suggested similar formats for organizing the sections of the report. Seagull (1979) recommends a more complex organizational format that includes Reason for Referral, History, Behavior, Assessment Procedures Used, Results, Interpretation, Conclusion and Recommendations, and Summary sections. Hollis and Donn (1979) also recommend a somewhat more complex structure, suggesting Report Identification, Client or Situation Identification, Purpose of Report, Psychological Data, and Summary as sections for reports.

These citations do not exhaustively review authorities' recommendations about report organization. They illustrate the substantial consensus that can be found—Klopfer and Huber, who were writing in the early 1960s, and Tallent, Seagull, and Hollis and Donn, all of whom were writing in the late 1970s, agree on the essential organizational format: The report's sections should include identifying information, a discussion of the reason for the assessment, a review of information sources, interpretation of the results, and a summary.

Perhaps one reason for this substantial consensus is that this report format makes sense to the reader. Analyzing the format according to the guidelines of the expository process model and, in particular, the dictates of the given-new contract shows why it makes sense. The given-new contract stipulates that any element of the report must establish that something is shared in common with the reader—the given—and must provide new information to the reader about the shared referent—the new element. The organizational format of the report suggested here follows these stipulations closely. The given of the entire report is the client. The format authorities suggest establishes the given at the beginning of the report by including the client's name and identifying information. The given of the assessment is the reason for referral, which is established next in a section of its own. Additional information that needs to be shared prior to interpreting test results is usually provided at this point in the report.

After the given is clearly established, the writer can proceed to the new elements of the report—the assessment data and their interpretation. From the point of view of the given-new contract, then, the given elements at the highest level of the report's organization are the Identifying Information, Reason for Referral, and Background Information sections of the report. The new elements in the sequence, then, are the Assessment Results, Summary and Conclusions, and Recommendations sections. Thus, even at the highest level of organization within the report, the given-new contract cannot be violated; fortunately, the basic report outline recommended by virtually all authorities who have made a recommendation is consistent with the contract.

Report Formats

This section presents a review of report formats that moves from least complex (the business letter) to most complex (the lengthy narrative).

Before you begin to write, you may want to make one further outline, this time either outlining the paragraphs of the letter or briefly detailing the content of the sections of the report. Although it may be possible to work directly from the EPM worksheet and the listing of referral questions and answers (suggested in chapters 4 and 6), both the novice writer and the expert can benefit from the additional conceptual clarity induced by organizing the ideas to be presented in the report in an outline. As Woodford (1967) has suggested, there may be an intimate relationship between clear writing and clear thinking. Whatever report format you choose, and however you organize it before you begin to write, it is critical that you have a clear overall concept in mind before writing. (See chapter 6 for additional discussion of this issue.)

Letter

Probably the simplest way to communicate evaluation information is to write a letter. In this situation, the psychologist communicates an account of the relevant circumstances of the evaluation, findings, and recommendations in a simple narrative format. This approach is frequently used in medical settings and is probably the most appropriate mode of conveying psychological assessment information to medical personnel. Using a familiar format is one way of tailoring the report to its context. It may be the most effective means of communication, and its use can enhance the reader's perception of similarity between writer and reader, an element of interpersonal attractiveness related to the report's capacity to influence the reader. While typically brief (one to two pages), it allows for a concise description of the reason for evaluation, the way the evaluation was carried out and with what results, and the psychologist's opinion of what the recipient's role in the treatment of the client should be.

Exactly what information should be included in the letter is up to the writer. Because brevity is essential, the choice of information ought to be guided by its relevance to the letter's intended recipient or the need to include it in order to substantiate the recommendations for treatment. A brief introductory paragraph that identifies the client and the reason for evaluation is a must; beyond that, the writer must decide what each individual report requires.

It may be helpful to include a statement that explains why information is being communicated if the reason is not immediately obvious, even if the referral was made by the report's intended reader. Medical personnel may be in contact with hundreds of clients in a short period of time, and it may not always be possible for them to recall quickly who the client is and why the client was assessed. Statements such as "Suzy was referred at your request for evaluation of her behavioral difficulties," or "I am writing at the request of Ms. Smith, who believes that this evaluation information may be useful in helping you to understand her son Joey" can refresh the recipient's memory or help the recipient understand and accept the communication of information that he or she may not have requested.

Evaluation information itself can be presented formally or informally depending on the situation. Even though physicians and other probable recipients of the letter are highly trained professionals in their own fields, their knowledge of psychological assessment procedures may be limited. Therefore, it is often best to describe the client's performance concretely in terms of its functional significance rather than to report tests and scores; it is also better to keep the use of middle-level constructs to a minimum. An example of this sort of interpretive statement is "Mary performed poorly on a measure that required that she repeat series of orally presented digits (WISC-III Digit Span subtest scaled score = 4, or the 2nd percentile). This suggests that Mary's difficulties in understanding oral instructions in the classroom may derive at least in part from difficulties in attention or short-term memory." The construct *short-term memory* is itself concrete and is illustrated thoroughly by the accompanying example.

When the assessment data have been communicated adequately to the letter's recipient, the writer should make a statement of his or her planned activity with respect to the client and, when appropriate, his or her opinion of what the other professional's actions might be. This latter statement should be made discreetly because professionals vary greatly in their willingness to accept advice from other professionals. A tactful follow-up phone call may be a better way to explore recommendations, particularly when the person who is receiving the letter is not well known to the writer.

The question may arise of whether a letter adequately serves the purpose of documenting assessment results. The answer to this question must be that sometimes it does and sometimes it does not; the purpose of the assessment and the length and detail of the letter must supply the answer to this question. In deciding whether to prepare a more detailed report, the psychologist must judge whether a letter will adequately communicate the nature and results of the assessment and the recommendations that stem from it.

Brief Narrative Report

In at least one study (Littlejohn, 1977), potential report recipients preferred the narrative report to other formats. The brief narrative report with recommendations, supported by face-to-face consultation when possible, is probably the format of choice for communicating most psychological assessments. This format allows for a concise yet complete description of the assessment process and for an extensive set of recommendations. Once the writer becomes accustomed to it, the brief format can easily be dictated or written in an hour or less. It will serve the purposes of communicating the assessment results, documenting the assessment for future use, and making written recommendations to those who are working with the client. Detailed explanation of assessment efforts can be provided orally during consultation, and the report can even be written in part from notes taken for the conference.

The sections of the brief narrative report will be familiar to most psychologists and are the same as for the lengthy narrative report. The difference between these two formats is, essentially, the degree of detail presented in each section. The brief report is usually no longer than two single-spaced typewritten pages, exclusive of recommendations. The writer should aim for less than one and a half pages; then there will be adequate space for any additions.

This economy of length can be achieved in several ways. First, the author of the report should have a clear idea of what he or she wants to say in the report—here again, the model worksheet, the referral questions worksheet, and a section-by-section outline can be useful in clarifying what is to be reported. While the psychologist may find it easy to write a great deal about test results, it may be far more difficult to succinctly report the information requested by the referring agent. Voluminous reports, while personally gratifying displays of professional diagnostic skill, are often useless to the persons who receive them. (Exceptions to this rule are noted below in the section on the lengthy narrative format.) If the essence of an assessment cannot be communicated in five to seven well-written paragraphs, the author should ask him- or herself whether he or she has sufficiently developed an overall concept of the evaluation results prior to writing.

A suggested outline for the sections of the narrative report is presented in Figure 7.1. The sections of the report include the given elements at the beginning of the report: identifying information, reason for referral, and background information. The remaining sections of the report consist of its new elements: assessment results, summary, diagnostic impression, and recommendations. Thus, the sections of the report include a brief introduction that details the reason for the assessment and provides pertinent background information. This section deals explicitly with defining the referral problem and placing it in

I. Reason for Referral

- data-based statement of the reason for referral
- specific statement of the question to be answered

II. Background Information

- discussion of previous evaluation results
- school, medical, or social history
- other pertinent information as needed

III. Observations

- behavioral observations during testing
- home, classroom, or playground behavior

IV. Assessment Results

- list of assessment tools with abbreviations
- results in tabular or narrative form

V. Summary and Recommendations

- statements integrating MLCs
- statements linking conclusions to recommendations

Figure 7.1 Sections of the Narrative Report

context, as discussed below. The rest of the report provides a narrative discussion of how the assessment was carried out (to the extent that such a discussion is necessary) and the results, conclusions, summary, and recommendations.

The following discussion assumes that you have worked through the model and referral questions worksheets and are now writing the outline of the report proper. The preliminary section of the report outline guides you in reconsidering the context of the referral. Ask yourself whether the context is simple or complex. For example, did the various persons who are working with the client agree on the purposes of the assessment? Are the client's physical and social environments factors that should be taken into account in the report? Are there important differences between the ways in which various professional personnel work with the client? Are there differences between settings, as with two different clinics or between a child's home and school?

Next, you should ask, "What—precisely—is the referral problem?" At this point, it may be useful to consider all aspects of the problem, both cognitive and behavioral. If the client manifests a cognitive problem, what is its impact on the client's ability to function? Persons with certain neurological disorders, for example, may exhibit memory deficits that preclude their moving about the community independently. Children with learning deficits are often unable to function in the regular educational environment. Thus, problems that appear purely cognitive in nature can have important effects on how the client functions behaviorally.

A third consideration in the preliminary outline is to note, however briefly, what the referring party wants from the assessment and to work toward satisfying this desire to the extent appropriate. This includes a consideration of any discrepancy between the report's message and the referral agent's own beliefs as well as the congruence of your report with the agent's agenda. Can you or should you cater to the agent's beliefs and agenda, in light of the possibility that the recommendations may not be followed if they are not at least somewhat congruent with the referral agent's agenda? If there will be a discrepancy between recommendations that result from the assessment and the referral agent's wishes, what steps can you take to help the report have maximum impact rather than simply being disregarded? Finally, you should determine what sort of style and format are correct in this particular context, taking into account the characteristics of the referral agent, problem, and environment.

At this point, you may object that these preliminaries will consume too much time and effort. You may ask, "Why add difficulties to an already arduous task?" It is likely that much of the arduousness of report writing comes from the fact that the writer has not adequately organized assessment results in an overall concept before beginning to write. The process of translating your ideas into written English is far simpler when the ideas are formulated clearly. As previously noted (Woodford, 1967), the relationship between clear thinking and clear writing may be interactive. Taking a few moments to consider the points discussed in the model and referral questions worksheets and to write a preliminary section outline will facilitate and shorten rather than impede and lengthen the process of writing the report.

Sections of the report. After consideration of these preliminary issues, you can turn to the content of the various sections of the report. The outline suggested in Figure 7.1 includes notations of the types of information that should be included routinely in the appropriate sections of almost every brief narrative report. While the information recommended for inclusion in Figure 7.1 is almost always required, the placement of particular items may be left to the writer's discretion. The sections presented here are, as noted, consistent with current practice and other authors' recommendations.

The report should include a section that lists information necessary for identifying the client and psychologist, and other data that may be needed for record-keeping purposes. This information typically includes: the client's name, address, and telephone number; in the case of an evaluation of a child, the child's parents' names, especially if their last name is different from the child's; the client's birthdate and chronological age; the dates on which the person was assessed and by whom; and a case identification number if one is used.

The report proper begins with a section headed Reason for Referral. This section should include a brief statement that indicates who made the referral and for what reason. The reason for referral is to be stated as specifically as possible. It may be useful to quote from the referral form and from the referral agent's statements during a preassessment conference. Ideally, the reason for referral will be stated in relation to observable behaviors without mediating interpretations. A statement such as, "Dr. Psyche referred Mr. Client because he states that he often feels anxious and depressed" is preferable to "Mr. Client was referred because of emotional difficulties." Here, the referral question is tied to something that can be observed—the client's statements that he often feels anxious and depressed. The model stresses the importance of making certain that statements about the client are based on data; this is no less true in the Reason for Referral section than it is in later interpretive sections.

This section should conclude with a brief statement of the referral questions as reformulated after reviewing the reason for referral. The reason for referral in the example above was the client's complaint that he often felt anxious and depressed. The referral question, as the summary statement of the Reason for Referral section of the report, could then be expressed as: "The questions to be answered in this evaluation are what might account for Mr. Client's feelings and what can be done to help him." Such a summary statement closes the preliminary section stylistically and gives the reader a clear idea of the purpose of the assessment.

Although it may be possible to consolidate the Background Information section with the Reason for Referral section, it is usually preferable to make these two separate, even though brief, sections. This makes the report more visually appealing by breaking what might be one long section into two shorter ones. Other information relevant to the assessment should be included in the Background Information section. This information might include a review of the results of previous psychological evaluations and other medical, physical or occupational therapy, or speech and language evaluations. Relevant information about the client's family or home situation can also be included here, although extreme tact and consideration for the client's privacy dictates that you be convinced that the inclusion of such information is necessary and will be beneficial. Important but sensitive information, such as that about family relationships, can be communicated to others orally when its inclusion in the report is probably inappropriate.

Hearsay (data known only by another's report) should be labeled clearly as such by attributing it to the person from whom it was heard. This helps avoid the problem of converting someone's casual observation or opinion into fact by merely presenting it above a psychologist's signature. A physical description of the client is an archaic practice to be avoided except when the client's physical characteristics materially affect the evaluation. In such cases, it is best to include a description of the client in the section on behavior and observations, as might be the case in reporting the evaluation of a severely retarded or orthopedically handicapped child.

The next section of the report may be headed Observations or Behavior During Assessment. This section can be omitted when there are no data that substantially affect the assessment. Statements such as "Mary's classroom behavior was appropriate" or "Mr. Client was pleasant and cooperative during test administration" add little to the reader's understanding of the person assessed and unnecessarily lengthen the report. When the psychologist notes defiant outbursts or inattentiveness during a classroom observation or anxiety and depression during test administration, a statement about the behavior's possible relationship to the referral problem should be made. Especially when the behavior occurs during test administration, the statement should include an estimate of the behavior's impact on the client's performance and the test's subsequent validity.

A frequent mispractice in this section, as well as in those following, is the presentation of isolated facts or behaviors that are not clearly linked to an indication of their significance. Behavioral observations may be reported, for example, without an explanation of their relevance to the client's functioning (as found by Ownby et al., 1982). Your task is not merely to present observations or test scores, but also to make them understandable to the reader and to elucidate their significance for the client's functioning. Every bit of data placed in the report should have a clear link to a middle-level construct, either by contiguous placement or through the larger structure of the surrounding narrative. Classroom observation of frequent failures to stay on task, for example, might be linked to the construct *distractible* as follows: "Paul's frequently observed inability to stay on task suggests that he is distractible."

The next section of the report is headed Test Results. The results are presented either in tabular and narrative form or, more simply, in narrative form alone. The reporting model (hypothesis-, domain-, or test-oriented) will affect the organization of this section. While it is common to present test results in tabular form at the beginning of the section, there is little justification for this practice because it encourages the reader to ignore the interpretation of the scores that follows and tends to overemphasize the importance of numbers in isolation from the client. While it is true that many recipients of reports want and are able to interpret test scores, you should consider whether test scores are reported in this fashion for a reasoned purpose or simply through habit.

When test scores are not presented in tabular format, they can be used in the narrative section of the report after you have presented a list of tests and other measures used in the assessment at the beginning of the section. A useful technical detail in relation to this list is in the inclusion of a test abbreviation after each element in it as a reference for later interpretations in the report narrative. If the list includes the element *Wechsler Adult Intelligence Scale–Revised (WAIS-R)*, later references to the *WAIS-R* will be readily understood by the reader. This is a particularly important practice when unusual measures are included in the assessment or when the report's intended recipient may not have a working knowledge of psychological testing. Test scores, expressed in a form appropriate to the report's reader, can thus be placed directly in the body of the report or in parentheses after a statement about them. For example, you might say, "John scored in the average range on the portions of the WISC-III that tap general verbal abilities (Verbal IQ = 95)." This method of referencing the middle-level construct (general verbal abilities) to data (Verbal IQ = 95) emphasizes the practical significance of the test score and, by its structure, subordinates the IQ itself to its relevance to the child's functioning.

How you divide the narrative of assessment results into sections depends on the orientation of the report. The test-oriented report may have paragraphs with headings for each test, which usually move from measures of intellectual ability to academic achievement, personality, and behavioral assessments. Domain-oriented reports can be organized around headings that name the domains judged relevant by the report writer. Such headings might include discussion of visual, auditory, linguistic, or personality domains. The hypothesis-oriented report may eschew sections completely and rely on a statement of the hypotheses and several supporting paragraphs, or it may be organized by test or modality. In this organizational format, the statement of the hypotheses might be followed by a consideration of support for the hypotheses from each test or in each modality. In this format, the sequence of the model constituents is reversed, with constructs being followed by data.

It was noted above that certain types of information may differentially affect the reader's perceptions of the client and of his or her ability to deal with the client's problems. The Test Results section should include a balanced report of the client's strengths and weaknesses in order to avoid making the reader pessimistic about the client's ability to improve and the reader's ability to help the client. Remember that information about why a client has a problem may lead the reader to have a more sympathetic view of the client. This type of information might be emphasized in reports when the client and the referral agent do not have a good rapport.

The final section of the brief narrative report, headed Summary and Recommendations or Integration and Recommendations, provides a brief overview of the assessment results, a statement of general conclusions, and a set of recommendations. The first paragraph in this section should provide a logical transition from test data to recommendations by summarizing constructs introduced in the test data section. This transition may be facilitated by discussing the implications of the assessment for the client's functioning and the relevance of the findings to work with the client. For example, the first paragraph of the section might begin, "Assessment results thus show that Mr. Client is so severely depressed that he is unlikely to benefit from psychotherapy until his mood improves." Recommendations that follow this statement could then suggest that Mr. Client be hospitalized or placed on antidepressant medication as a prelude to his receiving psychotherapy.

Before you list specific recommendations, it is sometimes helpful to include a second paragraph that states general strategies that may be useful in working with the client. For example, Mr. Client's report might include the following general strategy recommendation: "Mr. Client has a history of unhappy and hostile relationships with professionals. In general, it will be helpful to work with him in a way that does not emphasize the differences between him and the professional staff, such as using nontechnical language and treating him as an equal." In reports that deal with how to teach a client educational material, it may be useful to provide suggestions about general instructional strategies for work with the client. Such a recommendation might be, "This assessment suggests that, in general, a linguistic rather than phonics-oriented approach to reading instruction may be helpful in teaching Tommy to read." This content is consistent with Keogh's (1972) suggestion that assessments that focus on learning processes rather than on psychometric deficit may be most useful to educators.

Including statements of this sort in this section helps the reader make the logical transition from middle-level constructs and conclusions in the Assessment Results section to the recommendations. Another example of this sort of transition would be to move from assessment data showing that a child has a strong preference for visual strategies in reading to a suggestion that reading instruction might focus on the development of such strategies (in addition to others). Specific recommendations could, in turn, suggest activities for developing a larger sight word vocabulary with the child.

The narrative report concludes with the recommendations sections. The length of this section depends on the assessment outcome, the referral problem, and the referral agent's needs for specific guidance. In this fashion, then, the summary and recommendations section moves logically from a summary of middle-level constructs to conclusions and recommendations.

Lengthy Narrative Report

The lengthy narrative format is simply an expanded version of the brief narrative. In this approach, you can give free rein to your diagnostic acumen and provide the reader with an exhaustive discussion of assessment data. This format interacts with the contextual variables (referral agent, problem, and environment). The lengthy narrative report is most appropriate for the referral agent who has an interest in detailed explanations of psychological test data, such as another psychologist or a special educator. Referral problems that pose highly specific questions can best be addressed in a hypothesis-oriented report, but when the referral objective is to provide a general description of a client's functioning, the lengthy narrative may be appropriate. Finally, a complex referral environment in which many persons may read the report can dictate that a brief report be written, but when the environment is simple and the referral agent is likely to be interested, the lengthy narrative format may be used.

Recommendations Only

This format allows written transmission of recommendations without accompanying confidential test data. This approach is a partial and not altogether satisfactory solution to the problems of requests for written recommendations and the necessity for safeguarding confidential assessment information. This format may be particularly useful in a highly complex referral environment in which it is difficult to be sure precisely who will be reading the report. This format is usually not used in isolation, but in conjunction with one of the other formats. In practice, it might be possible to distribute copies of the recommendations at the same multidisciplinary staff meeting at which assessment results are presented.

Summary

This chapter has presented a discussion of several formats for report organization with suggestions for content in each section. Ways of using each of the formats to communicate assessment results in different contexts have been discussed, and recommendations about specific content for each section of the report have been made. Although this discussion has presented the report formats as though they are distinct entities, in practice you may find that you develop a hybrid report format for use in your own setting. Alternatively, you may find that one of these formats works for most of your assessment reporting and that you do not have to change your report format frequently.

8

SPECIAL PROBLEMS IN THE SPECIALTIES

This chapter presents a discussion of problems in reporting that are more likely to be encountered by those working in the various specialty areas of psychology. The applied specialty areas considered here include the four traditionally recognized by the American Board of Professional Psychology—clinical, counseling, school, and industrial/organizational—as well as two of the new specialty areas—neuropsychology and forensic psychology. The problems encountered by persons who work in these areas are representative of the sorts of problems likely to be encountered in any of the specialties; persons who work in other specialty areas, such as pediatric or health psychology, are likely to find material in a number of the following sections relevant to their work.

A common issue that affects reporting in the applied specialties is that psychologists are frequently called on to communicate with persons in other professions, such as medicine or law. Psychologists must be able to function in at least two professional worlds, each with a unique approach to defining and solving problems. This can have major implications for writing reports. In no specialty is this more true than in forensic psychology, where the legal and psychological definitions of terms such as *insanity* or *competence* may be quite different.

The differences between specialty area reports and typical psychological reports, and between reports in different specialty areas, can be classified along a number of dimensions, mainly related to the purpose of the report. Reports written by clinical psychologists for other clinical psychologists, for example, may be quite different in content, organization, and style from reports written by forensic psychologists for attorneys. The following sections briefly review what makes each specialty different from the others, discuss the implications of these differences for report writing, and give suggestions about how to deal with problems that are likely to arise in the settings in which each specialty functions.

Clinical Psychology

Clinical psychology traditionally has been concerned with assessment and remediation of disordered behavior (American Psychological Association, 1981). Clinical psychologists have often worked in psychiatric settings such as those that exist in the Department of Veterans Affairs hospital system; today, they are often found working in medical contexts as well as in community and university settings.

The implications of this specialty's focus are that clinical psychologists are likely to work with persons who have long-term disabilities and to work in settings that are more medically oriented than other specialties of psychology. It is particularly likely that clinical psychologists will work closely with psychiatrists, psychiatric nurses, and psychiatric social workers because many of the clients clinical psychologists see also require interventions by these specialists. Clinical psychologists who are writing reports in these settings should, therefore, be prepared to write reports that will be intelligible to highly trained medical specialists.

It should be noted in particular that while psychiatrists and other medical personnel may be familiar with personality theory, classic and modern conceptions of psychopathology, and both traditional and recent approaches to psychotherapeutic intervention, they may not be equally familiar with psychological testing. Medical personnel may not always understand the basic statistical concepts that are crucial to the interpretation of tests. While basic medical information about a client might be mentioned only briefly in a report for a medical professional, it may be necessary for the psychologist to provide extensive discussion of basic concepts in psychological testing. In this situation, the pacing of the writing should be adjusted so that the more technical information is explained in greater detail and, hence, at a slower pace.

Fewer details are needed for material with which medical professionals are likely to be familiar.

Another implication of clinical psychology's traditional focus on disordered behavior is that clinical psychologists are often asked to carry out detailed assessments of a client's personality functioning. This raises the issue of writing reports in language that will be appropriate to the report's intended recipient. For example, a report written in psychodynamic language that emphasizes the client's drives, defenses, and symptoms probably won't please the behaviorally oriented clinician. Thus, it is necessary for the clinical psychologist who is carrying out assessments for psychologists of different theoretical orientations to be able to communicate assessment findings in ways that the other psychologists will find useful and meaningful. This often requires adjusting the way in which middle-level constructs are used and the way other aspects of the report, such as model and format, are approached.

A referral problem likely to be encountered frequently in clinical psychology is assessment for psychotherapy. In addition to a consideration of problems such as anxiety, depression, or behavioral disturbances, such an assessment usually involves an extensive examination of the client's functioning in order to determine his or her ability to profit from psychotherapy. Here, it is critical for the clinical psychologist to be familiar with the referral agent's theoretical orientation. As noted, a dynamically oriented report may be virtually useless to a behaviorally oriented clinician.

It is in this area that the middle-level constructs of clinical psychological reports may differ from those of other specialties. Hollis and Donn (1979, pp. 41–61) discuss how the theoretical orientation of the psychologist should influence the psychological report. They present a few basic concepts about the impact of theoretical orientation on report writing that are likely to be true for most psychologists, whatever their specialty. First, Hollis and Donn suggest that every writer recognize that he or she has a personal theoretical orientation that affects how he or she writes reports. Explicit consideration of this personal orientation may help the writer to avoid expressing in reports personal assumptions that may not be held in common with the report's reader. Second, they suggest that the writer integrate his or her theoretical orientation toward personality and treatment to write a report that is similarly integrated. A theoretically integrated report will be more likely to make sense to the reader.

Third, Hollis and Donn suggest that the report writer should modify his or her writing on the basis of an understanding of the theoretical orientation of the report's intended recipient. Although some might argue that the writer is being dishonest if he or she writes a report that is inconsistent with his or her own beliefs, Hollis and Donn argue that, "the purpose of the psychological report is to communicate—not to wage philosophical wars" (p. 43). In the following sections, constructs pertinent to a number of theoretical orientations are presented in conjunction with discussion of how to utilize them appropriately.

Theoretical Orientations

What follows is not intended to be a complete listing of the theoretical orientations of psychologists. Some of the major areas of counseling and psychotherapy theory are discussed in order to provide examples, and the effects of each orientation on the report are illustrated. If the theoretical orientation you are interested in is not discussed, it may be possible to generalize from these examples and apply the principles illustrated in your own writing.

Psychodynamic

In a report written for the psychodynamically oriented psychologist, the writer may be required to discuss the meaning of projective and objective personality assessment data and present an explanation of the client's central drives, conflicts, and defenses. The writer may be expected to explain the relationship of scores on ability measures to the client's personality functioning as well as to provide dynamic explanations for the client's behavior during the interview and testing administration.

Constructs likely to be useful in this assessment include several key concepts in dynamic psychologies, such as *drive, conflict,* and *defense.* It is particularly important to keep the report's reader in mind when you are working with these concepts because even sophisticated readers may not agree on what a term such as *rationalization* means. As always, it will be best to provide substantial amounts of data to illustrate the meaning of the concept. The term *obsessiveness* might be rendered, for example, as "the client's tendency to worry excessively about insubstantial details," or the term *denial* might be explained as "the client's ability to assert that something is not true, even when faced with compelling evidence to the contrary." The following passage is from a psychodynamically oriented report about a client referred for evaluation by his therapist because of the client's classic Type A behavior pattern:

> Results of objective and projective personality measures indicate that Mr. Strongarm is conflicted about several dynamically important issues, including dependency needs and sexual identity. He has dealt with these conflicts by developing an exaggerated masculine identity in which he demands absurdly high levels of performance from himself both at work and even in sports activities in which he engages ostensibly so that he can "relax." His primary defense against anxiety, when the character structure that he has constructed so carefully is threatened, is to verbally act out. Psychodynamic psychotherapy with Mr. Strongarm is likely to be stormy because formation of the therapeutic relationship itself will threaten to expose Mr. Strongarm's strong needs to depend on and be cared for by another person.

This example shows that it is possible to construct a report that can provide useful information about a client's dynamics without using terms such as oral needs or reaction formation. The dynamically oriented psychotherapist will almost certainly be able to understand what is said in this report, and so will other, less sophisticated readers.

Behavioral

The report written for the behaviorally oriented therapist should communicate information about those aspects of the client's functioning that will provide the clinician with useful information in developing a behavioral intervention. Thus, the report will not focus on internal dynamics, as did the report for the dynamically oriented clinician, but on the relationship of the client's maladaptive behaviors to the responses of the client's environment.

Constructs useful in communicating with the behaviorally oriented clinician include terms such as *reinforcement, contingency,* and *behavior modification treatment strategy.* Communicating assessment data in these terms is likely to make the report more useful to the clinician. Here is an example of a behaviorally oriented report on Mr. Strongarm:

> Results of this assessment show that a number of factors in his environment may reinforce Mr. Strongarm's maladaptive behaviors. His socially inappropriate aggressiveness often elicits reinforcement from his environment in the form of others acquiescing to his demands. When he aggressively demands of a subordinate that a task be done in the particular way he wishes, the subordinate is likely to do exactly what Mr. Strongarm demands. This pattern of behavior can also affect Mr. Strongarm's relationship with his spouse, who may often respond to his aggressive behavior by acquiescing, even at the cost of her own wishes. Interventions with Mr. Strongarm might focus on altering the contingencies in his environment with respect to his maladaptive behavior. It might be possible to encourage others around Mr. Strongarm simply to ignore his inappropriate aggressiveness and, thereby, subject it to extinction.

Here, the report focuses not on Mr. Strongarm's internal states, but on the effects his inappropriate behaviors have on his environment. Suggestions for interventions, therefore, also focus on the environment in finding possible strategies for altering the response contingencies that impinge on Mr. Strongarm's behaviors.

Cognitive

The report for the cognitively oriented clinician should focus on elucidating what cognitions underlie the client's problematic behaviors. Therapists who are particularly interested in the Rational-Emotive Therapy (RET) developed by Albert Ellis (Ellis & Grieger, 1977) might desire an explanation of the client's tendency to catastrophize about minor happenings or of the "shoulds, oughts or musts" that the client says to him- or herself, which in turn, lead to unsatisfying behavior. Clinicians interested in the theories of Aaron Beck (1976) might desire an explanation of the ways in which the client overpersonalizes the events around him- or herself.

Cognitive constructs include a variety of terms specific to the theory of the therapies. Persons trained in RET may attach special significance to the client's "should" statements and be quite interested in how the content of such statements may affect his or her behavior.

An example of a cognitively oriented report on Mr. Strongarm follows:

> Results of this assessment suggest that several cognitive distortions affect his behavior. Mr. Strongarm believes that it is critical to his happiness in life for him always to be right, always to win, and always to be the best. When these irrational beliefs are threatened by life events, he becomes anxious or depressed and reacts to these emotions with a consistent pattern of excessively competitive behavior and compulsive overwork. Related aspects of Mr. Strongarm's behavior are his near-constant smoking and occasionally excessive use of alcohol as health-damaging attempts at stress management. Treatment with Mr. Strongarm logically might focus on helping him understand and modify his irrational belief system. A related intervention would be to help him develop and implement a stress management program.

Phenomenological

Another distinct group of therapies are those based on phenomenological methods, including the person-centered therapy of Carl Rogers (Rogers, 1961), Gestalt therapy (Perls, Hefferline, & Goodman, 1951), and existential psychotherapy (Yalom, 1980). In contrast to the other therapeutic approaches discussed, the phenomenological therapies are concerned to a greater extent with clients' own perceptions of the world and the ways in which they give meaning to events in their lives. Rather than the objective approach of dynamic, behavioral, or cognitive therapies, phenomenological therapies emphasize the subjective experience of the individual. The central implication of this is that reports for the phenomenological therapist should focus primarily on clients' experience of the world and the relationship of their perceptions to their behaviors. While a general description of client personality might consist of a detailed discussion of drives and defenses for the dynamic therapist, for the phenomenological therapist it should consist of a detailed explanation of how the client perceives him- or herself in the world and the ways in which these perceptions contribute to problematic behaviors.

Constructs in phenomenological therapies vary by therapeutic school. Person-centered therapists may be especially interested in the way the client experiences him- or herself and in the client's willingness to risk new experiences. Gestalt therapists are most likely to want data on the client's typical distortions of interpersonal contact, termed *resistances* by Gestalt therapists. Existential therapists may be most interested in information on how the client deals with the basic issues of existence—loneliness, fear of death, and bringing meaning to his or her life. Constructs such as these are most likely to be useful in communicating with phenomenologically oriented therapists.

Here is an example of a report on Mr. Strongarm prepared for a phenomenologically oriented therapist:

> Results of this assessment indicate that Mr. Strongarm's problematic behavior may stem from basic anxiety about fears of loneliness and the lack of meaning in his life. Even though his interpersonal behavior suggests a large and varied social life, Mr. Strongarm derives little true satisfaction from these contacts. He himself says that when prevented from engaging in his very active lifestyle, as when ill, he feels empty inside and quite lonely. Although he is strongly committed to work and social activities, when he reflects on these things, he views many of them as meaningless. Thus, therapeutic work with Mr. Strongarm might focus on helping him become more aware of the ways in which his denial of anxiety has affected his behavior by impelling him into a pattern of overwork and excessive competition with and hostility toward others. Therapy then might progress toward helping Mr. Strongarm develop a lifestyle that he experiences as more authentic in terms of his true self.

Clearly, writing for the phenomenologically oriented therapist requires familiarity with the basic concepts of the therapeutic modality. Even such common terms as *anxiety* may have a special meaning to the phenomenological therapist—in this case, the word anxiety is related more closely to Kierkegaard's philosophy than to Freud's (Brenner, 1957). In a similar way, the term *authentic* has a meaning based in the philosophical writings of Heidegger (1949).

Although the clinical psychologist will write reports about many other topics, one that he or she is likely to encounter with some frequency is the topic of assessment for psychotherapy. This section has argued that the psychologist should be able to couch the assessment report in terms that will be meaningful to the therapist who receives it. You can imagine what might happen if you were to send the phenomenologically oriented report above to a strictly behaviorally oriented clinician; this should serve as a reminder to tailor your language to the report's intended recipient.

Counseling Psychology

Counseling psychology as a specialty of professional psychology is usually concerned with the task of helping those who are already functioning adequately to function better, often in the face of normal developmental events that cause temporary maladjustment. Another task that has been addressed specifically by counseling psychologists is the assessment and reporting of vocational interests and abilities (American Psychological Association, 1981).

The implications of this focus are that although the report still addresses the client's personality and need for counseling, it will do so from the perspective that the client's difficulties are temporary and that they may have resulted from normal developmental events. Consider the case of a college freshman who is experiencing difficulties in adjusting to life in a dormitory. The freshman may need guidance with dating skills, time management, and study skills—concerns that are far different from those addressed by the clinical psychologist in the inpatient psychiatric setting.

Another implication is that the counseling psychologist may be called on to communicate with other professionals about clients' interests in vocations and their ability to succeed in them. Few other professions have extensive knowledge of the basic concepts that underlie the vocational groups or vocational choice as a developmental phenomenon. This fact may require the counseling psychologist to spend some portion of the report dealing with vocational issues or explanations of the meaning of a particular pattern of interests. It might be necessary to explain, for example, that an artistic pattern of interests on a vocational interest measure does not necessarily mean that the client should become a studio artist. A related problem is explaining to those who are naive about vocational interest assessment that interest patterns are closely related to other aspects of personality function. Clearly, the person with a strongly conventional interest pattern will behave quite differently from the person with an artistic pattern. This sort of information may be useful to the report's intended recipient.

Constructs in counseling psychology are those attached to consideration of behavior problems as normal developmental phenomena and to assessment of vocational behavior. Reports might include terms such as, *developmental issues, stress-related problems, clerical speed and accuracy*, or *realistic interest pattern*. As with clinical psychology, these terms have specific meanings to those trained in the specialty, and the report writer should be familiar with the terms and their underlying theory before attempting to write a report of the assessment.

The following passage illustrates how behavior problems can stem from normal developmental difficulties. The client, Christina, is a 19-year-old freshman at a large state university:

> Results of this assessment show that Christina's depression is probably the result of adjustment difficulties here at Large State University. This is her first protracted experience of being away from home, and she feels overwhelmed by the tasks that confront her. In addition to adapting to the large classes and increased academic task demands, she has to make new friends and deal with dating issues. Interventions with Christina might focus first on helping her simply become aware that her problems are common to persons in her situation, so that she does not feel depressed merely because she has these difficulties. Second, it may be useful for her counselor to help Christina develop a time management plan. This program might have the dual impact of helping her manage her time better and at the same time helping her feel more in control of her life. It may also be useful for Christina to participate in one of the study skills workshops offered at the campus counseling center. Third, assertiveness training interventions might help Christina learn to deal more effectively with her roommates. Fourth, helping Christina develop skills for dealing with the issues of dating would be a substantial help in reducing her anxiety about her relationships with men. Ongoing

contact to support her during this time of adjustment is recommended.

Counseling psychologists work in a number of settings besides college counseling centers, including hospitals that provide rehabilitation services. In such settings, the counseling psychologist might be asked to write a report about a client's vocational interests and abilities after treatment for medical and psychological problems. The following client, Rick, is a 32-year-old veteran who has been treated successfully for posttraumatic stress disorder and related substance-abuse problems:

> Results of this assessment suggest that Rick might be encouraged to explore occupations in manual trades such as carpentry, metal work, welding, or other building trades. Rick's pattern of vocational interests suggests that he will prefer occupational activities that allow him to work with his hands in accomplishing something visible, such as constructing a building. Assessment of abilities and academic skills shows that Rick probably has the prerequisite skills to profit from a training program or formal apprenticeship. Rick's own statements support the test data in suggesting that these are areas that might be explored profitably. For example, when asked what he liked about previous occupational experiences, Rick immediately related how he enjoyed building with wood in the Army and in his shop classes in high school. Rick's rehabilitation counselor may find it helpful to work with him in exploring these types of work and in locating possible training programs.

Here, basic test data on occupational preference and ability have been translated into a plan that encourages the reader to help the client further develop his interests in and knowledge of specific occupations without explaining vocational choice theory at length. In addition, note that statements in the report are referenced to concrete examples.

Thus, writing a report in counseling psychology reflects the particular concerns of this specialty with assisting clients in dealing with normal developmental and vocational adjustment tasks. The report's constructs, content, and style reflect the concerns of the specialty by using terms drawn from the theories that underlie each area of endeavor and a manner of expressing ideas consistent with the issues often addressed by the specialty.

School Psychology

School psychology as a specialty has traditionally been concerned with the child in the educational environment. Although school psychologists have adopted other roles, including counselor, consultant, and organizational specialist, an important continuing focus of the work of the school psychologist during the last several years has been the individual assessment of children who are not functioning well in school.

The implication of this for reporting is that reports must focus on explanations of how a child's learning and behavior patterns influence his or her success in school. More, perhaps, than in other specialties, detailed analyses of learning patterns and of their interaction with the child's successful acquisition of academic skills are content for reports. The child's social-emotional or behavioral status also becomes important content for reports, particularly when it impinges on the child's classroom functioning. Another implication of school psychology's tradition of providing services in schools themselves is that the psychologist has a working relationship with other educational specialists, including regular and special education teachers, reading specialists, and school administrators. These are the specialists with whom the school psychologist will communicate most often: Knowledge of their vocabulary and way of looking at children's problems is, therefore, essential.

Middle-level constructs in school psychology follow logically from these emphases. Their content usually deals with ability and achievement, central concerns of most school psychological assessments. Although school psychologists are by no means all behaviorally oriented, many are accustomed to working with behaviorally based interventions and programs. They will be less interested in dynamic interpretations of a child's behavior than clinical or counseling psychologists. Behavioral data on which an intervention might be based are more likely to be useful to the school psychologist.

The following is a passage from a school psychological report:

> Results of this assessment suggest that John's academic failures in the first grade may be due to specific learning difficulties. Although his scores on measures of general ability indicate that he is probably functioning in the high average range of general intellectual ability,

his scores on measures of academic achievement are much lower. It appears possible that a severe discrepancy exists between John's ability and his achievement and that he may be eligible for special educational services. These results will be brought to the attention of the school district's placement committee.

This brief passage illustrates the common concern of school psychologists for assessment data from measures of ability and achievement. The rest of the passage highlights two other important factors that affect the way the school psychological report is written. First, scores from school psychological assessment are often used in part to determine whether a child can receive special education services. Second, the passage illustrates that the psychologist must often communicate test scores to other educators on a placement team, who will then determine as a group whether the child in question is eligible to receive special education services. These two factors require that the psychologist be particularly accurate and appropriate in representing test scores in reports because they are used in making a decision that can have enormous impact on the future of the child assessed. Special education placement procedures are regulated by state and federal laws; in no other psychological specialty does legislative regulation have such an important effect on the psychologist's day-to-day functioning.

Industrial/Organizational Psychology

One traditional focus of industrial/organizational/(IO) psychologists has been on the evaluation of current and potential employees in work settings. Although many I/O psychologists today are involved in activities other than individual psychological assessments, reporting assessments of employees is still an important function.

Here, the implications of this focus include the role of the report in communicating with business professionals and the pressure for concrete and clear answers to management decision questions. Managers may not be sympathetic to reports that include much hedging about the validity of the measures used for prediction of employee behavior (although the psychologist's duty to the employee and the organization requires that the psychologist be clear about the limits of the psychological assessment in predicting employee success or, perhaps more importantly, employee failure). Beyond answering the basic question of whether a person might be successful in a particular position, the psychologist who is evaluating employees might provide management personnel with additional useful information about the employee's strengths and weaknesses in order to help guide their decisions about the employee in the future.

Constructs in I/O psychology follow from the concerns of the specialty. Discussion of ability is usually limited to overall intellectual skill levels and to the basic academic skills necessary to perform particular types of tasks. Usually, discussion of personality function is also limited primarily to personality characteristics relevant to work with employees. In assessing management personnel, for example, one might discuss the person's concern for the welfare of subordinates, need for achievement, or capacity for good working relationships with others from divergent backgrounds as aspects of personality functioning that are clearly related to the person's capacity to function as a manager.

An illustrative passage from an I/O psychological evaluation follows:

> Results of this assessment show that Jones is likely to be successful in the position of department manager. She possesses good intellectual skills and the capacity to work well with others. Personality assessment shows that she is likely to be able to combine a strong concern for task accomplishment with an appropriate level of concern for her subordinates. Her preferred decision-making style is to gather data, to reflect for a substantial time, and then to act on the basis of her thinking; when confronted with time limits, however, she is able to make decisions without losing her poise, and there is no evidence that the quality of her work deteriorates.

This report illustrates several characteristics of the I/O psychology report. Its style is less complex than that of reports in the other specialties, in keeping with the no nonsense attitudes of many business managers. Issues are addressed directly in a way that does not allow the psychologist the opportunity to clarify minor ones. The clinician accustomed to addressing the fine points of personality function or test interpretation may be uncomfortable with the directness and apparent conviction of this style, but in business (and in law, as discussed in the section on forensic psychology) the reader of the report is primarily interested in brief direct answers to the referral question and may be annoyed and frustrated by the psychologist's well-meaning attempt to write the assessment report as though it were addressed to another psychologist.

Clinical Neuropsychology

Clinical neuropsychologists are employed in a number of settings, the most common of which are general medical and psychiatric facilities. Their primary task is to communicate assessment findings—indeed, many neuropsychologists do not engage in treatment activities at all. Neuropsychologists usually work with patients who have actual or suspected neurological disorders. They are frequently attached to the departments of neurology or psychiatry in medical facilities, where they may work with patients with degenerative neurological diseases, head injuries, or psychiatric disorders, or with children who have learning or behavior disorders.

Because assessment is their primary task, clinical neuropsychologists are often under pressure to write many reports quickly. They are also pressured by the need to communicate the results of extensive test batteries to highly trained medical specialists. Thus, neuropsychologists are required to quickly report the results of a large number of tests to persons in another profession, usually medicine. This combination of circumstances means that the neuropsychologist may be able to use very technical medical terms, but be forced to deal with concepts in psychology at a rudimentary level.

The neuropsychologist also writes reports for persons in other specialties. Depending on the clientele with whom he or she works, the neuropsychologist's reports will be read by other psychologists, speech pathologists, occupational or physical therapists, and rehabilitation counselors. In addition, reports written about children with learning or behavior difficulties may be communicated to school personnel. With such diverse potential report recipients, the report writer must be particularly cautious unless he or she knows the referring agent well.

Constructs in clinical neuropsychology emerge logically from the types of symptoms that persons with neurological disorders, broadly defined, may present. Problems with learning and memory, for example, are often a concern, and neuropsychologists frequently engage in exhaustive assessment and reporting on memory function, using terms such as *verbal* and *nonverbal memory, short-term versus long-term memory, retrieval,* and *storage.* These terms have fairly specific meanings to most psychologists, but the report writer should be aware that the relative precision of the terms' meanings in psychology is not echoed in other professions. Here, as in virtually all other situations, the psychologist should be cautious, referencing constructs to behavioral observations or test data contained in the report.

The following example illustrates several of these difficulties in reporting the neuropsychological assessment. The client has a neurological disorder that affects her left temporal lobe:

> Results of this assessment show that Ms. Smith's complaints of memory failures are based on functional difficulties in both storage and retrieval of verbal material. Her ability to learn a list of 12 words, for example, was clearly impaired because she was only able to repeat 6 of them after the list was read to her five times. This level of performance was probably not due only to difficulties in retrieving the words from memory because her recognition memory (assessed as her ability to pick out the words previously read to her from a list of words) was also impaired—only 8 correct, while a normal performance would probably be a perfect 12. Assessment of Ms. Smith's nonverbal memory for geometric figures and her incidental memory for a formboard she worked with when blindfolded indicates that her memory functioning in nonverbal areas is probably within normal limits. It may be useful for Ms. Smith to return for additional work in the cognitive rehabilitation program in our department.

This report does not assume that the reader is at all sophisticated about psychological measurement. Concrete examples of the client's performance are provided each time an evaluation of performance is given. Particularly when reporting the results of learning measures, it may be useful to couch the results in terms of percentages. Many readers will not see immediately the practical implications of a client's remembering only of 6 of 12 words, but when the report writer states that the client remembers only 50%—or one half—of what he or she learns, they can quickly see that the test performance may point to a significant functional disability.

Forensic Psychology

Forensic psychologists are primarily concerned with the individual whose behavior has brought him or her into direct contact with the legal system. They may be called on to assess whether a person with a mental disorder is competent to cooperate in his or her defense, whether a person knew the difference between right and wrong at the time a crime was committed, whether a person is ready to be released or moved to a less restrictive treatment environment, or whether a person is likely to repeat an offense after being released. Forensic psychologists often engage in professional activities other than assessment, such as psychotherapy and consultation, but reporting the results of psychological assessments remains an important part of their work.

Forensic psychology, perhaps more than any other specialty, requires that the psychologist modify his or her approach to language usage in reports. This is because the forensic psychologist operates within the judicial system, in which particular words and phrases are given precise meanings and in which important unwanted consequences may arise if these meanings are not apprehended. The precise meaning of the phrase *reasonable certainty*, for example, varies between the federal and state court systems as well as among the states. Psychological constructs, even though identical to words or phrases in law, may have different meanings. The legal definition of *insane*, for example, may vary across localities and may be quite different from the meaning that most psychologists would give it. Lawyers, more than any other professionals, are in the business of using language in technical ways. The rules of language usage in law are determined by a tradition that extends back at least to the time of the Magna Carta; psychologists who are working in the legal system must acquire a familiarity with the ways lawyers use language if they wish to write reports that will be useful to the persons assessed as well as in the judicial decision-making process.

Examples of other constructs in forensic psychology include terms such as *incompetent, mentally ill,* and *probability*. These terms may have definite legal meanings that can differ from what the psychologist might assume. In these cases, the psychologist simply must be sure that he or she understands how the courts in a particular jurisdiction use them. Referencing constructs to behavioral observations and test data assumes a new importance in the practice of forensic psychology. Here, the psychologist is not simply striving to convince the probably sympathetic reader. In forensic psychology, the psychologist's statements may be subjected to tests of proof that are similar to those demanded of other witnesses. Even though the psychologist's report will be submitted as expert opinion, he or she may be required to explain in detail how a conclusion was reached if called on to testify in a courtroom proceeding. If he or she has already made reference to the basic assessment data in the report, subsequent statements in court may appear more consistent—an important factor in the psychologist's credibility as an expert witness.

The following report illustrates some of these issues. The report is written about a 23-year-old woman who attacked a stranger on the street and who now stands trial for assault.

> Results of this assessment show that Ms. Brown did not understand the nature of her acts at the time of their commission. She also states that the person she attacked was a "devil" and that she had to destroy the man or risk coming under his control. She states that if she had come under his control, he would have compelled her to engage in sexual acts that to her would have been disgraceful and personally disgusting. Ms. Brown's history of hospitalization for mental illness is consistent with this pattern of symptoms. On two prior occasions she has voiced concerns that others could control her and make her do things that were obscene. Because Ms. Brown was raised in a rather rigid moralistic home, her concerns about being forced to engage in sexual acts are even more exaggerated. It is, therefore, my opinion that Ms. Brown was mentally ill at the time of the incident and that she was not able to control her actions at that moment. It is also my opinion that she continues to be mentally ill and will be for the foreseeable future. She will probably require psychiatric care for an extended period in the future, such as might be provided at State Psychiatric Facility, where she now resides in a security unit.

This report illustrates the types of information that are likely to be communicated in a forensic psychology report. The client's mental status at the time a crime was committed is likely to be of interest to the court because a determination of the client's guilt or innocence often depends on establishing whether he or she knew right from wrong or was able to control his or her actions at the time of the crime. The court is also likely to be interested in the psychologist's opinion about the client's future functioning and needs for treatment. In the example above, the psychologist was able to predict with reasonable certainty that the client would continue to require hospitalization and psychiatric care. The judge might take this suggestion into account when disposing of the case by requiring the client to remain in treatment at a particular facility while the judge is given periodic progress reports about the client's improvement.

Summary

This chapter has shown that certain aspects of good report writing are consistent across specialties. The need to write clearly and to reference constructs to assessment data is present in every specialty. Although not a comprehensive guide to reporting in each specialty, these examples illustrate the ways in which the alert report writer can modify his or her approach according to the demands of the situation.

9

EXISTING RESEARCH AND FUTURE NEEDS

Chapter 1 presented an outline of reporting variables. In this chapter, the outline will be reviewed considering the material presented throughout the book. This review shows which issues about report writing have been empirically investigated and what guidance these studies can give. Figure 9.1 reprises Figure 1.1 for your reference.

Structural Variables

Several variables have been assessed at the structural level. Research shows that statements are probably more effective when they are constructed in the form dictated by the expository process model. Three studies (Ownby, 1984, 1986a, 1990b) show that statements are rated more positively when constructed with the model, regardless of the type of referral problem (cognitive versus behavioral), the type of data used to support the statement (test versus observational), or the setting in which the raters are employed (schools, community mental health center, state hospital, or university). These results provide substantial support for the usefulness of the model in psychological report writing.

These same studies show several interesting results about the contents of isolated statements. The study of the model with school psychologists (Ownby, 1990b) obtained a significant interaction of model by problem type. This result shows that it may be especially important for writers to support behavioral constructs with assessment data.

> ### Results of Research
>
> I. STRUCTURAL VARIABLES
>   A. Sentences
>   B. Paragraphs
>   C. Sections of the report
>
> II. ORGANIZATIONAL VARIABLES
>   A. Models
>   B. Formats
>   C. Style
>
> III. CONTEXTUAL VARIABLES
>   A. Referral agent
>   B. Referral problem
>   C. Referral environment

Figure 9.1   Outline of Reporting Variables

Another finding about the content of statements (Ownby, 1986a) was that statements based on test data were rated significantly more positively than were similar statements based on observational data. A related finding was that statements that utilized inferences about children's cognitive behavior based on observations were rated less positively than statements based on authors' judgments. Although counterintuitive, this shows that readers may find that an explicit indication that the evaluator has used his or her judgment suggests that he or she is trustworthy. It should be noted, however, that test data as evidence were always rated more positively than any other form of basic data. Conclusions from these studies suggest the following guidelines for report writing:

1. Use the *expository process model* to construct sentences.
2. Be particularly careful to support statements about clients' behavioral functioning with raw data.
3. Use test data as the most, and observational data as the least, useful types of data.

At the level of the paragraph, the model has also fared well in at least one research study (Ownby, 1990a). Paragraphs constructed on the basis of the model were virtually always preferred as more effective by a diverse group of report readers. Integration of content, structure, and problem variables has not been investigated. This leads to the following guideline:

4. Use the *expository process model* to construct paragraphs.

At the level of the sections of reports, structure and content variables have not been investigated extensively. Several studies indicated a strong consumer preference for the traditional format, however (Pryzwansky & Hanania, 1986; Wiener, 1985, 1987; Wiener & Kohler, 1986). In chapter 4, it was noted that the traditional report format is consistent with the guidelines of the given-new contract. Given this research support for the application of the model at the levels of sentences, paragraphs, and indirectly at the level of organization, it appears reasonable to hypothesize that the basic underlying principle of the model—the given-new contract—can be applied effectively here as well. Application of the model to sections within the report requires that paragraphs establish certain facts from the assessment as givens before they are used as shared referents in a succeeding paragraph and that the sections of the report follow a logical sequence as well. Hence, the following guideline:

5. Use the principle of the *given-new contract* in constructing the sections of the report and in guiding its overall organization.

The theory of reporting practices associated with the comprehensive outline illustrated in Figure 9.1 predicts that the structural variables should be invariant across organizational and contextual variables. Studies reviewed to this point provide limited support for this prediction. Model-based statements and paragraphs are consistently rated positively by psychologists who are working in divergent settings, including schools, community centers, and inpatient hospitals. At this time, however, no more explicit tests of this prediction have been carried out.

Organizational Variables

Little research can be cited to provide recommendations about organizational variables. Authorities almost always agree that some report characteristics should be tailored to the context within which the report will function, but they have seldom made detailed or specific recommendations. In the comprehensive outline, the report variables that are postulated to interact with context variables are model, format, and style. Review of opinion suggests the following guidelines with respect to these variables:

6. Use the hypothesis- or question-oriented *model* when reporting assessments undertaken primarily for a narrowly focused issue. Use the domain-oriented model when you are reporting assessments undertaken for broader purposes.

7. Choose a *format* that reports the necessary information in the shortest, simplest, and clearest fashion possible.

8. *Model* and *format* probably interact. Use briefer formats with hypothesis-oriented reports, and longer formats with domain-oriented reports.

9. Although the professional *style* discussed in chapter 5 should be used throughout the report, formality and other aspects of style should vary depending on the relationship between report writer and reader. The closer the relationship, the more informal the style may be, within the limits of the professional purposes of the report.

Although the theory predicts that internal-organizational variables should interact with contextual variables, little direct evidence supports this prediction. Indirect support comes from the finding that improvement in feedback mechanisms between referral agent and report writer results in improvement in reports' rated usefulness or effectiveness (Affleck & Strider, 1971; Hartlage & Merck, 1971; Ownby & Wallbrown, 1983).

Contextual Variables

Here again, little direct research evidence can be cited to provide guidance to writers. Review of authorities suggests the following guidelines with respect to contextual variables:

10. Assess the *referral agent's* profession, level of training, openness of agenda, and your relationship with the agent and tailor the report accordingly.

11. Assess the *referral problem's* type and degree of clarity. Try to make the referral problem as clear as possible. Review the problem type and tailor the report accordingly.
12. Assess the *referral environment* to determine whether there is only a primary reader or whether the environment includes diverse secondary readers. Tailor the report accordingly.

These, then, are the central guidelines that result from detailed consideration of the writing on psychological reports. Although there are only twelve, it is likely that your report writing will be substantially improved if you implement them in practice. Using them will require, for example, that the structure of your sentences, paragraphs, and report sections be data-based and that the conclusions and recommendations you make in the report follow logically from your interpretation of the data. Implementing these guidelines will also ensure that you assess the report's context and tailor the report's organization accordingly.

Areas for Future Research

The outline in Figure 9.1 helps point out what types of research remain to be done to test the theory of psychological report writing. Several structural variables have already been studied. Making recommendations about how to write sentences, paragraphs, and the sections of reports is now possible, and how best to use content can also be specified. Much work remains to be done, however, to better establish that structural variables are invariant across context. Testing the effects of content variables on statements' effectiveness might also be useful. For example, assessing whether the effectiveness of statements using observational data is improved when they also include test data might be helpful.

Another area that merits consideration is finding out whether structural variables affect readers' beliefs and behaviors. Although a close relationship probably exists among ratings of credibility and belief and behavior change, failing to show this relationship is a serious weakness of studies done to date. A design that could address this issue would be to ask readers to rate an imaginary client on scales predicting the client's behavior after readers have seen several types of reports. This design would also allow study of the interactions of type of information in the report with type of belief change. You may recall that Schwartz's (1977) study showed that different types of information affected readers' perceptions of clients in different ways. Although work remains, structural variables are the best researched of the three categories of reporting variables.

Research on organizational variables and their interactions with contextual variables has not gone as far. Although studying organizational and contextual variables independently of each other could be useful, some organizational variables clearly interact with some contextual variables. Research on these variables will be most fruitful if it examines the interactions among and the main effects associated with each variable. One potential study could focus on interactions of report formats with professional and environmental complexity. Research might assess the preferences of several professional groups for different report formats. Raters' attitudes could be changed by emphasizing that the report deals with either a specific question or a broad description of the client. Based on previous studies, it is likely that preferences for report organization would vary by profession and by the function of the report.

Determining the effects of feedback on report writing and client treatment is particularly important. Although the importance of feedback has been shown in at least one study (Hartlage & Merck, 1971), little information has accumulated on the ways in which feedback affects reports. Research on this topic could provide empirical tests of one of the theory's basic ideas: that reports are most effective when organizational variables change with contextual variables. Because feedback is the best mechanism by which this covariance can happen, a study of this process may be essential in understanding reports.

Computers in Reporting

Using computer assessment and reporting is the focus of several publications (Adams & Heaton, 1985; American Psychological Association, 1986; Brown, 1984; Burke & Normand, 1987; Fowler, 1985; Hartman, 1986; Jacob & Brantley, 1987; Kramer, 1988; McCullough & Wenck, 1984; Skinner & Pakula, 1986; Thomas, 1984; Walker & Myrick, 1985). There has been a virtual explosion of articles on the subject of computers in assessment; most have focused on a combination of three general topics: (a) providing readers with general information about the availability of computerized assessment systems; (b) expressing concerns about the statistical properties of computerized test administration and scoring systems; and (c) expressing concerns or making specific statements on the ethical issues involved in computerized assessment and reporting.

These topics are germane to report writing; certainly today most psychologists are aware of the potential for using computers to automate assessment activities. Users of computer-based reporting services should be aware that most reports generated this way have not demonstrated their validity. As Matarazzo points out, "To date, there is no evidence . . . that one page of the narrative descriptions is valid" (1983, p. 323; also see Matarazzo, 1986). This highlights the fact that although computers can be useful in scoring tests and computing various scores and indices, interpretation of test scores remains a task for the psychologist even when the computer provides a number of interpretive hypotheses.

The psychologist must interpret test data in the context of other assessment variables, such as client demographic characteristics, history, and other test results. Psychologists who use computerized systems should treat results from them as a professional-to-professional consultation in which the validity of particular interpretations is assessed by the psychologist who has direct contact with the client. Until computer-based interpretive systems are considerably more advanced, psychologists must use the results of these programs with caution. Under no circumstances should a computer interpretation be included in a report unless it is clearly supported by assessment data or clearly labeled as speculation. To produce reports at less than this standard risks unethical behavior. As Walker and Myrick point out, "Users of psychological test interpretation programs or services should be cautioned *not* to view the output of these computerized programs as psychological reports, and certainly not as the final report" (1985, p. 54).

Another computer-related issue stems from the treatment of the expository process model in chapter 4. This presents the possibility that the algorithm for sentences and paragraphs inherent in the model might be used by computerized interpretive services to produce effective statements in computer-generated reports. Because the model guidelines are quite specific, a personal computer could be used in conjunction with the model to create EPM worksheets or even preliminary drafts of reports. The writer could then edit the machine-produced text. This use of computers is certainly defensible. It amounts to an automated writing service because interpretation of test data remains solely the responsibility of the writer. Thus, applications of the model or the comprehensive outline present intriguing, but as yet unrealized, possibilities.

Reporting Activities Other Than Assessment

This book has focused explicitly on reporting assessment activities, partly because this function is central to most psychological specialties and partly to limit the discussion to a manageable area. Most psychologists in everyday practice do, of course, report other activities besides individual client assessments. Examples of such reports vary from recording the progress of therapy in notes to writing lengthy research reports. While it is possible that the elements developed in the context of assessment reporting—the given-new contract, the expository process model, the comprehensive outline of reporting practices, and the theory—might be expanded to other areas of reporting such an expansion would require substantial additional theoretical and research development.

Conclusion

In this book I have tried to present in distilled form the results of my colleagues' and my own searches for the best way to report psychological assessments. The general lack of empirical research and the absence of specific evidence about important issues is a problem. As research continues to produce answers to the question, "How do I write the best psychological report?" psychologists move closer to the time when reports will be better grounded. Perhaps then this area of psychological practice will receive the attention it deserves.

APPENDIX A:
LEARNING THE
MODEL

Writing Sentences

As discussed in chapter 3, writing sentences with the model requires recognizing two elements: (1) a *given*, often the client, and (2) a *new*, often the results of an assessment procedure. The given and the new can be related to each other through various grammatic constructions. Elaboration, contrast, and the absolute contruction are illustrated in chapter 3. What follows are several more examples for practicing the skills of using the model to write sentences. These are drawn from actual reports, with information changed to protect the client's identity. Note that the sentences you construct in this section will be used in the next section to construct paragraphs. It is probably best to write down your responses, but at least try a few of these examples if only by working them out mentally.

The following data refer to a 6-year-old boy named Morris. Data for each proposed sentence are provided, with suggested answers at the end of each section.

#1   GIVEN: Morris

     NEW: WISC-III Verbal IQ = 96; Performance IQ = 77; Full Scale IQ = 85. Combine these elements into a sentence by reporting the ranges into which the scores fall (Verbal = average; Performance = borderline impaired; Full Scale = low average).

Going further with Morris's WISC-III data, the subtests were reorganized and rescored to provide factor deviation quotients. Combine these into a sentence or sentences:

#2 GIVEN: Morris

NEW: Verbal Comprehension IQ = average; Perceptual Organization = borderline impaired; Freedom from Distractibility = borderline impaired.

Another test administered to Morris was the Bender Visual-Motor Gestalt Test. Combine the following information into a sentence or sentences about these results.

#3 GIVEN: Morris

NEW: Performance was significantly below age-based expectations.

NEW: Type of errors suggested impulsivity and poor fine motor skills.

Assessment information need not always derive from tests. Sometimes, information also may arise from informal inventories or interviews. What follows are several bits of information derived from varied sources during assessment of Mary Riley, a 65-year-old referred for evaluation because of reported memory problems:

#4 GIVEN: Mary

NEW: Could not state her age

NEW: Could state the year of her birth

Here are additional data derived during assessment of Ms. Riley.

#5 GIVEN: Mary

NEW: Could state the name of the current U.S. president

NEW: Could not state the name of the previous president

NEW: Could not state the name of the current state governor

And here are still more data.

#6 GIVEN: Mary

NEW: Stated that the year was 1968 (it was 1995)

NEW: Said she was unsure of the month

Answers

You should recognize that no one will produce exactly the same sentences from these data and that there are many correct ways of reporting test results. The following sentences are offered as suggestions.

#1: Although Morris's performance on the portion of the WISC-III that primarily taps verbal skills was in the average range, his performance on the portion that taps visuospatial skills was in the borderline impaired range. The overall result is an IQ score in the low average range. (Full Scale IQ falls in the range 79–91.)

#2: When the subtests of the WISC-III are recognized according to the specific abilities assessed by groups of subtests (factor analytically derived deviation quotients), his score on the verbal portion was in the average range, while his scores on the perceptual and attentional skills sections were in the borderline impaired range. (Note that the Freedom from Distractibility score may be interpreted in several ways; see Ownby & Matthews, 1985.)

#3: Morris's performance on a measure of his visual-motor skills assessed as his ability to copy geometric forms with pencil and paper (Bender) was significantly below age-based expectations. In addition, the types of errors that he made on this task, which suggested impulsivity and poor fine motor skills, were relevant to his school learning problems.

#4: Ms. Riley was unable to state her own age, although she was aware of the year in which she was born.

#5: She could report the name of the current president of the United States, but could not say who was the president before him, nor could she say who is the current governor of the state.

#6: She stated that the year was 1968 (it was 1995), but was unsure of the month.

Writing Paragraphs

By using the given and new elements in the last section, you have constructed a group of sentences about two different clients. In this section, you can use these sentences to construct two paragraphs about new clients. You may remember that two types of paragraphs were illustrated in chapter 4. The Type I paragraph consists of a topic sentence that includes middle-level construct, data, and a conclusion that summarizes and explains the significance of the findings. The Type II paragraph consists of a topic sentence without a middle-level construct, data, and a conclusion that includes a construct. The Type I paragraph emphasizes the importance of the data for the client, while the Type II paragraph emphasizes the importance of the construct, which may be a diagnosis or may allow the inference of significant clinical symptoms.

Try organizing the data provided above into a paragraph or paragraphs about Morris. This task will also give you the opportunity to try your hand at integrating data from two measures.

Answers

Again, it's possible to arrive at many different correct ways of narrating the data provided. What follows is a suggestion.

Results of this assessment show that Morris presents with an unusual ability pattern consistent with difficulties in visuospatial abilities, attention skills, and planning. Although his performance on the portion of the WISC-III that primarily taps verbal skills was in the average range, his performance on the portion that taps visuospatial and manual skills was in the borderline impaired range. This pattern of abilities is consistent with difficulties in many academic subjects, such as letter and word recognition skills, as well as difficulties in completing classwork. When the subtests of the WISC-III are reorganized according to the specific abilities assessed by groups of tests (factor analytically derived deviation quotients), the pattern is still clearer. For example, Morris's score in the verbal area is in the average range, while his scores in the perceptual and attentional skills areas are in the borderline impaired range. These results are thus consistent with substantial perceptual and attentional deficits.

This psychometric impression is strengthened by inspection of

Morris's performance on a measure of visual-motor skills assessed as his ability to copy geometric forms with pencil and paper (Bender). Morris's performance on this measure was far below age-based expectations; in addition, he showed many errors of a type often found among children with learning or attentional deficits.

Sentences 4, 5, and 6 above provided assessment data on Ms. Mary Riley, referred for memory problems. Try organizing those data into a paragraph. A suggested answer follows:

Answers

Ms. Riley presents with significant difficulties in recent memory and orientation. For example, she was unable to state her own age, although she was aware of the year in which she had been born. She could name the current president of the United States, but could not say who the previous president was nor who is the current governor of the state. In orientation, also, Ms. Riley was impaired. She stated that the year was 1968 (it was 1995) and was unsure of the month.

Organizing the Sections of the Report

As discussed in chapters 2 and 5, the use of the traditional sequence of sections in the report is supported both on theoretical and empirical grounds. Rather than provide large sections of several reports for you to organize, possible sentences from each section of the report are provided. Your task is to determine in which section of the report they should be placed. Answers are provided below.

Decide whether the following statements should appear in the Identifying Information, Background Information, Test Results, or Recommendations sections:

1. Results of this assessment show that Pat probably is functioning in the average range of general intellectual ability (IQ range = 90–110).
2. Patrick Woodrow, 2341 Anyplace Lane, City
3. Previous evaluations showed that Pat probably was functioning

in the low average range of general intellectual ability, prior to his receiving speech therapy services.

4. In spite of his obvious progress, it is likely that Pat will continue to benefit from special educational services.

5. Pat's scores on several measures of reading skills were at levels significantly below average (for example, Woodcock-Johnson Psycho-Educational Battery Reading cluster standard score = 65).

6. Assessment date: June 5, 1995; Psychologist: Childe Psychologist, Ph.D.; Case Number 640303.

7. Based on his pattern of performance on the Verbal and Performance portions of the WISC-III, it may be helpful to refer Pat once again for speech and language evaluation.

8. Pat received language therapy services during first and second grades, after which they were discontinued as no longer necessary.

Answers

(1) Test results; (2) Identifying Information; (3) Background Information; (4) Recommendations; (5) Test Results; (6) Identifying Information; (7) Recommendations; (8) Background Information.

APPENDIX B: DIAGNOSING PROBLEMS IN YOUR REPORTS

Now that you have read the book and had an opportunity to practice using the model (assuming you have worked through the examples in Appendix A), you may want to try to improve your own reports. This will require diagnosing specific problems with your own writing. This Appendix provides a number of suggestions for ways to improve the reports you already write; they are grouped in three areas: self-diagnosis, consumer feedback, and colleague feedback.

Self-Diagnosis

One of the best ways to diagnose problems with your reports is to dig into your files and look at reports you wrote some time ago. When reports are no longer fresh, you can read them with a more objective eye and see difficulties you might have missed when the reports were first written. Asking yourself the following questions may be useful in the self-diagnosis process. They derive from the recommendations of the expository process model and follow each of the sections of the traditional report format.

Identifying Information

Is the information supplied adequate to identify the client uniquely (e.g., name, case number, birthdate)?

Is other useful information supplied (e.g., address, telephone number, age, grade in school, school building, clinic site)?

Is information that helps identify the assessment supplied (e.g., name of the psychologist, date of evaluation)?

Is unnecessary, unimportant, or irrelevant information supplied?

Reason for Referral

Is this section included and, if not, is the reason for the evaluation adequately stated elsewhere in the report?

Is the reason for the referral explained clearly in this section?

Does the explanation include sufficient information so that a rationale for the assessment is clear?

Does the section include a one-sentence summary that succinctly states the reason for the evaluation (e.g., "The purpose of this evaluation was to determine Billy's eligibility for special education services." or "The purpose of this evaluation was to help the therapist better understand the reason for Mr. Wilbuthnot's apparently compulsive behavior.")?

Background Information

Is this section necessary? If not, can relevant information be shifted to another part of report?

What irrelevant information can be eliminated?

What information is necessary for understanding the reason for referral, results, or recommendations is omitted?

Observations

Is there a reason for this to be a separate section, or could observations be better integrated into the Assessment Results section?

Are observations sufficiently explained so that the client's behavior can be readily visualized or understood by the reader?

Are observations clearly related to the purpose of the assessment?

Are observations readily linked to later conclusions? Do you use foreshadowing appropriately when it is useful? (See glossary.)

Assessment Results

Are sources of assessment information listed or otherwise clearly identified?

Are professional terms used in this section? If so, are they truly shared referents?

Are any middle-level constructs that are not shared referents anchored to behavioral description?

Are sentences clearly given-new sequences related to the client?

Are paragraphs Type I, Type II, or some other form?

Are constructs used effectively to link assessment data to conclusions?

Is foreshadowing used when appropriate?

Is the referral problem clearly addressed, and are any relevant questions clearly answered?

Summary

Does the summary provide a restatement of all results relevant to the reason for referral and the recommendations that follow?

Is new information added in this section? If so, is there a compelling reason why it was not provided in the results section?

Does the summary provide a logical flow to the recommendations?

Is the referral problem clearly addressed in this section also?

Diagnosis

Is this section provided when necessary?

If so, is the diagnosis provided consistent with both the data included in the report and the diagnostic criteria used (e.g., DSM-IV)?

Recommendations

Are recommendations clearly tied to problem areas identified in the report?

Are the recommendations for each problem identified? If not, is a rationale for this omission provided in either the summary or this section?

Are recommendations explained in sufficient detail to allow the provider to carry them out?

Are unfamiliar or professional terms used in this section? If so, are they shared referents (e.g., "use a *linguistic approach* to reading instruction" or "use *reframing* with this client in psychotherapy")?

Are specific recommendations included that address the referral problem? If not, is a rationale provided either in the summary or in this section?

Are recommendations realistic? Do they conform with the possibilities inherent in the recipient's environment (e.g., classroom teaching or psychotherapy in a college counseling center)?

Overall

Is the report visually overwhelming? Are paragraphs longer than 10–12 lines?

Are sections, headings, and side headings used when effective?

Is the report neatly typed? Is it possible for the reader to quickly identify information about and answers to the specific referral problem? If useful, can the recommendations section be readily detached and circulated?

More on Self-Diagnosis

Study sentences. It may be useful to study intensively a few sentences drawn randomly from the report. Can you identify the given? Are there middle-level constructs, and, if so, are they linked to descriptions?

Study paragraphs. Take several paragraphs from your reports and identify the central topic for each. Are the elements included in each paragraph related to the central topic? If not, should they be placed elsewhere in the report, or deleted?

Consumer Feedback

Perhaps the simplest way to obtain feedback about your reports is to ask for readers' comments. This procedure, though, may not result in much useful information. The next best way to ask for feedback is to ask consumers to complete a brief questionnaire. All the following questionnaires are based on the basic outline provided by Ownby and Wallbrown (1983). The questions in each of the following are updated and are tailored more closely to each group of consumers. The questions may vary, but each simply involves asking readers for answers to a set of questions.

School Personnel Questionnaire

This questionnaire is intended for use in school settings, to solicit information from teachers, counselors, administrators, and others.

EVALUATION FORM FOR PSYCHOLOGICAL REPORTS

We want to find out how helpful our reports are to those who receive them. We have written the following questions so that, if you are willing, you can give us information about whether this report was helpful to you and if not, why not. This information is very important in helping us improve our services.

1. Did the report answer the referral question?
   _____ Yes   _____ A little   _____ No

2. Did the report give you new information about the student?
   _____ Yes   _____ A little   _____ No

3. Did the report help you develop new ideas for working with this student?
   _____ Yes   _____ A little   _____ No

4. Were the recommendations about how to teach this child helpful?
   _____ Yes   _____ A little   _____ No

5. Were the recommendations about how to deal with the child's behavior helpful?
   _____ Yes   _____ A little   _____ No

continued

---

continued

6. Did the recommendations show that the person writing understood how a classroom operates?

_____ Yes   _____ A little   _____ No

7. Overall, how useful is this report?

___ Very useful   ___ Somewhat useful   ___ Not useful

8. What information should have been included, but wasn't?

_____

_____

9. What terms were unclear or seemed to be jargon?

_____

_____

10. What suggestions would you make for improving this report?

_____

_____

Parent Questionnaire

This questionnaire is intended for use with parents.

EVALUATION FORM FOR PSYCHOLOGICAL REPORTS

We want to find out how helpful our reports are to the parents who receive them. We have written the following questions so that, if you are willing, you can give us information about whether this report was helpful to you and if not, why not. This information is very important in helping us improve our services.

1. Did the report answer the questions you may have had about your child?

_____ Yes   _____ A little   _____ No

2. Did the report give you new information?

   _____ Yes   _____ A little   _____ No

3. Did the report offer new ideas for helping your child to learn better?

   _____ Yes   _____ A little   _____ No

4. Were the recommendations about how to teach your child helpful?

   _____ Yes   _____ A little   _____ No

5. Were the recommendations about how to deal with your child's behavior helpful?

   _____ Yes   _____ A little   _____ No

6. Did the recommendations show that the person writing understood the problems parents face in raising children?

   _____ Yes   _____ A little   _____ No

7. Overall, how useful is this report?

   ___ Very useful   ___ Somewhat useful   ___ Not useful

8. What information should have been included, but wasn't?

   _____

   _____

9. What terms were unclear or seemed to be jargon?

   _____

   _____

10. What suggestions would you make for improving this report?

    _____

    _____

Therapist/Psychiatrist Questionnaire

This questionnaire is intended for use in clinical or mental health settings, in which primary intervention is likely to be psychotherapy or medication. In clinical settings, data may be used to help therapists plan long- or short-term therapy or to help psychiatrists make decisions about symptom patterns, diagnoses, and medications.

EVALUATION FORM FOR PSYCHOLOGICAL REPORTS

We want to find out how helpful our reports are to those who receive them. We have written the following questions so that, if you are willing, you can give us information about whether this report was helpful to you and if not, why not. This information is very important in helping us improve our services.

1. Did the report answer the referral question?
   _____ Yes   _____ A little   _____ No

2. Did the report give you new information about the client/patient?
   _____ Yes   _____ A little   _____ No

3. Did the report help you develop new ideas for working with this client/patient?
   _____ Yes   _____ A little   _____ No

4. Was the discussion about what causes this client's/patient's difficulties helpful?
   _____ Yes   _____ A little   _____ No

5. Were the recommendations about therapeutic strategy or behavior modification helpful?
   _____ Yes   _____ A little   _____ No

6. Did the recommendations show that the person writing understood the limitations within which you must work, such as duration and frequency of therapy sessions?
   _____ Yes   _____ A little   _____ No

7. Overall, how useful is this report?
   ___ Very useful   ___ Somewhat useful   ___ Not useful

---

8. What information should have been included, but wasn't?

_____

_____

9. What terms were unclear or seemed to be jargon?

_____

_____

10. What suggestions would you make for improving this report?

_____

_____

Colleague Feedback

If you work in a setting with several other psychologists, your colleagues can be an easy and potentially helpful source of feedback. They can read your reports with an objective eye and cite examples in which your reports may be unclear or in which terms may be jargon. If you wish, you can ask one or several of your colleagues to complete the following questionnaire as well.

EVALUATION FORM FOR PSYCHOLOGICAL REPORTS

We want to find out how helpful our reports are to those who receive them. The following questions are designed to help us learn the extent to which we have been successful in communicating assessment results clearly and correctly. We have written the following questions so that, if you are willing, you can give us information about whether this report seems helpful to its intended reader, and if not, why not. Please also feel free to add any comments you have at the bottom or on the back of this sheet.

continued

---

continued

1. Did the report answer the referral question?
   _____ Yes   _____ Somewhat   _____ No

2. Did the report give you new information about the student/ client/patient?
   _____ Yes   _____ Somewhat   _____ No

3. Do you think that the report would help the reader to develop new ideas for working with this student/client/ patient?
   _____ Yes   _____ Somewhat   _____ No

4. Do you think that the discussion about what causes this student's/client's/patient's difficulties would be helpful to its reader?
   _____ Yes   _____ Somewhat   _____ No

5. Would the recommendations about therapeutic strategy, behavior modification, or teaching techniques be helpful to the reader?
   _____ Yes   _____ Somewhat   _____ No

6. Did the recommendations show that the person writing understood the limitations within which the reader must work, such as classroom procedures or the duration and frequency of therapy sessions?
   _____ Yes   _____ Somewhat   _____ No

7. Overall, how useful is this report?
   ___ Very useful   ___ Somewhat useful   ___ Not useful

8. What information should have been included, but wasn't?

   _____

   _____

9. What terms were unclear or seemed to be jargon?

   _____

   _____

10. What suggestions would you make for improving this report?

    _____

    _____

APPENDIX C:
A DICTIONARY
OF BEHAVIORAL
DESCRIPTIONS

Throughout this book, the use of behavioral descriptions in place of professional terms has been advocated. This appendix provides such descriptions for some major terms, tests, subtests, and scales that are likely to be used in psychological reports. Note, however, that these operationalizations may not be appropriate for every context; a definition of intelligence that emphasizes critical thinking ability may be more relevant in an employee evaluation than in a report about a child with severe developmental disabilities. For this reason, the following descriptions should be regarded primarily as examples of how specific terms can be made more intelligible to the average adult reader without professional training rather than as a cookbook of descriptions to be plugged into your report. Also for this reason, only one major instrument or group of instruments is illustrated in the areas of intelligence and personality assessment.

Intelligence

Wechsler Scales are a series of items arranged in order of increasing difficulty to compose subscales. Each set of items within a subscale taps a relatively specific ability or set of abilities. The overlap among the client's performances on all of the subtests is assumed to reflect his or her general intellectual capacity, although individual performances on subtests can be used to better understand specific assets and liabilities.

The *Verbal Scale* consists of subtests that tap the ability to understand, reason about, or explain the meanings of words. For example, the Information subtest taps the client's knowledge of a wide range of topics, while the Vocabulary subtests tap his or her ability to define the meanings of words. The *Performance Scale* includes subtests that tap visual reasoning skills or the ability to carry out tasks with one's hands. For example, the Block Design subtest requires that the client assemble geometric patterns with color plastic blocks, while the Object Assemble subtest asks the client to assemble puzzles of common objects.

Following are descriptions of each of the subtests of the Wechsler scales:

Information: This subtest may be described as tapping the client's knowledge of a wide variety of topics, which range from simple concepts about numbers to the discoveries of famous scientists.

Similarities: This subtest taps the client's ability to reason about the meanings of words, assessed as the capacity to say how two words are alike.

Vocabulary: This subtest taps the client's knowledge of what words mean by asking the client to explain them to the examiner.

Arithmetic: This subtest asks the client to solve arithmetic problems read aloud.

Comprehension: This subtest assesses the client's practical knowledge of what he or she should do in a problem situation, such as dealing with a lost child in a supermarket.

Digit Span: This subtest taps the client's ability to repeat a series of numbers.

Picture Completion: This subtest asks the client to identify missing parts in pictures.

Picture Arrangement: This subtest demands that the client arrange a set of pictures into a story that makes sense.

Object Assembly: This subtest asks the client to assemble puzzles of common objects.

Block Design: This subtest requires that the client assemble geometric designs with colored plastic blocks.

Digit Symbol, Coding, Animal House: Depending on whether the WAIS-R, WISC-III, or WPPSI-R is administered, this subtest may be described as a clerical task, a substitution task, or a task that requires visual-motor skills.

Symbol Search: This subtest requires that the client find things under timed conditions.

Personality

The Minnesota Multiphasic Personality Inventory (MMPI, MMPI-2) is a personality assessment measure that is based on relationships between the ways in which people respond to test items and the ways in which they have been observed to behave. High scores on scale 1, for example, are obtained by persons who have many concerns about bodily functions and may complain of a wide variety of vague illnesses. High scores on scale 2 are obtained by persons who are observed to be sad, "blue," or frankly depressed. Such persons may also be viewed by others as discouraged and pessimistic about the future.

Persons who obtain high scores on scale 3 are often described by their therapists as resistant to psychological interpretations of their difficulties. High scorers on scale 4 are described as manifesting hostility or anger; they are often described as having histories of difficulties with authority and histories of alcohol or drug abuse. Males who score high on scale 5 are described as having a pattern of artistic interests and to be interested in intellectual pursuits, while women with low scores on scale 5 are described as being strongly identified with traditional female roles. Persons with high scores on scale 6 are unusually sensitive to the opinions of others and at times may be frankly paranoid.

High scorers on scale 7 are described as highly anxious and inclined to think over their problems excessively. High scores on scale 8 are associated with persons who report unusual perceptual experience and who are viewed by others as unusual or as not fitting in socially. Persons with high scores on scale 9 are said to act frequently without thinking and to possess high energy levels. High scorers on scale 0 often do not enjoy socializing with others and may be described as shy or anxious around others.

The preceding descriptions, it should be emphasized, simply serve as brief descriptions of scales associated with clinical entities, such as depression and introversion. It also should be emphasized that each scale is associated with several meanings and that the preceding brief descriptions are not a substitute for thorough knowledge of the varying meanings of scales depending on clinical population and patterns of other scales. Graham (1982) is a good source for additional interpretive information.

APPENDIX D: EXAMPLES OF PSYCHOLOGICAL REPORTS

The four complete psychological reports included in this appendix illustrate ways to apply the principles discussed in this book in actual practice. The first example illustrates a brief report of a psychoeducational evaluation of a 5-year-old. Although in some instances a more lengthy report can be useful, this report communicates the essentials of the assessment in a way that allows persons who are working with the child to grasp the nature of his difficulties and the recommended course of action. The second example reports the assessment of a woman in an outpatient clinical setting; it shows how to address a specific request for a diagnostic opinion as well as a general request for treatment recommendations. The third example illustrates one of several approaches to reporting neuropsychological assessments, in this instance, the assessment of a child with an unusual neurological disorder. Its Recommendations section is particularly lengthy in response to specific requests from the referring psychologist. The fourth example is the report of a court-ordered assessment in a forensic setting; it shows how to address specific questions from the court and to provide treatment and placement recommendations.

All four reports were actually used in their respective settings; names, dates, and specific data have been changed to protect the clients' anonymity. The last three represent somewhat lengthy reports of the expanded narrative variety—they are longer than the page and a half recommended in chapter 7 because they represent specific responses that require a considerable degree of detail. It is hoped that by showing how the principles of report writing are applied to real assessment problems you will be better able to apply them in your own work.

Report I: Psychoeducational

This example reports an assessment undertaken to help a public school district's placement team determine the most appropriate educational setting for a preschooler. Essential data gathered by the psychologist consistent with the school district's policies included data on the child's overall intellectual functioning (Stanford-Binet), visual-motor skills (Developmental Test of Visual-Motor Integration), and educational skills (Woodcock-Johnson). The recommendations in this report are brief and general; they reflect the report's focus on providing a general description of the child and specific test scores rather than on in-depth diagnostic evaluation. This report can be contrasted with the third report in this section, which includes detailed recommendations for managing a child's behavior and academic problems. Also note that this report includes a diagnosis section, a requirement of the agency for which this report was produced.

PSYCHOLOGICAL EVALUATION

Name: Michael Smith
Address: 3311 Pine Bluff City

Case No. 123456
Date of Birth: 2-5-91
Chronological Age: 5–9

Reason for Referral

Michael was referred by his teacher in the Therapeutic Preschool Class, Ms. Winona Goodstreet, who requested additional test data in order to facilitate placement decisions by the Public School District. Michael has participated in the Therapeutic Preschool Class during the past two years, and his teachers report that he has shown substantial improvement in his language skills and ability to maintain attention on educational tasks.

Michael's developmental history is significant for having been delivered by Caesarean section and having in the past been treated for a seizure disorder. At the present time, he is not on medication.

Previous evaluations in February and November suggested that Michael probably functions in the high average range of general intellectual ability (IQ range = 110–120), but that his behavior was at times a problem. Evaluation showed that Michael was sometimes described as defiant toward adults and that he has a low frustration tolerance. His diagnosis at the time of the present evaluation was attention-deficit/hyperactivity syndrome.

Speech and language evaluation in February showed that Michael displayed a mild to moderate receptive language delay together with problems in auditory discrimination of speech sounds.

Assessment Results

Measures used:

Stanford-Binet Intelligence Scale, 4th Edition (SB-IV)
Developmental Test of Visual-Motor Integration (VMI)
Woodcock-Johnson Psycho-Educational Battery (WJPEB)
Draw a Person (DAP)

Results of this assessment suggest that Michael is functioning in the average range of general intellectual ability. Although his composite score on the Binet was in the range 75–83, this score may be slightly lower than Michael's actual presentation because his performances on abstract/visual reasoning and quantitative tasks were lower than the potentially more relevant score on the verbal reasoning section. Here, his score was in the range of 99–111. His score on the short-term memory section of the Binet was in the range of 85–97.

Assessment of Michael's visual-motor skills as his ability to copy geometric forms with pencil and paper suggests that he displays a relative deficit in this area. Michael's grasp of the pencil was awkward, and he displayed minimal ability to copy the forms of the VMI (score = 2nd percentile).

Brief assessment of the development of Michael's preacademic skills shows that he has developed the ability to recognize some letters on sight, but at this time he does not read any complete words. He has also developed basic number concepts, including rote counting and the ability to associate numbers less than five with the same number of objects.

Assessment of Michael's behavioral status through projective drawings (DAP) and observation in class and during test adminis-tration suggests that he continues to display a great deal of poorly modulated activity characteristic of children with attention deficits and hyperactivity. In addition, his behavior suggests poor impulse control as well as general difficulties in cognitive organi-zation. Although he appears both bright and perceptive, at times it was difficult to obtain his cooperation during test administration. It appears that even though Michael may want to please adults, his difficulties with attention and distractibility may make it difficult for him to do so. It is likely that he will display behavioral difficul-ties in large group situations, such as the typical kindergarten class.

Summary and Recommendations

Results of this assessment continue to show that Michael prob-ably functions in at least the average range of general intellectual ability in verbal areas. When his skills in quantitative or visual reasoning areas are assessed, however, his resulting perfor-mances are at lower levels. This may be due to his general perceptual disorganization, most evident in measures of his visual-motor skills. His difficulties in impulse control and planning also contribute to these relatively lower performances.

Results of this assessment show as well that Michael should be considered a candidate for special class placement when he begins to attend public schools, as may be determined by the school district's placement committee. It is apparent that even though he has made great progress in the Therapeutic Preschool Program, it is unlikely that he will be able to succeed in a large group situation without special attention. A suggested area of educational remediation is his visual-motor skills, which reflect a broader disorganization of visual perceptual abilities.

Diagnostic Impression

Axis I: Attention-Deficit/Hyperactivity Disorder, Combined Type
  (314.01)
Axis II: No diagnosis on Axis II
Axis III: Deferred

_____

Signature

Report II: Adult Clinical

This report addresses several common problems encountered in work
in clinical settings. The client was referred by her therapist in a community mental health center for treatment recommendations; the consulting psychiatrist also requested specific diagnostic information. The
Reason for Referral section makes it clear that both requests are to be
addressed.

_____

PSYCHOLOGICAL REPORT

Name: Jessie Smith   *Case No.* 11223344-0
Address: 2020 Anystreet,   *DOB*: Month, day, year
Thistown, State   *CA*: 39–6
Telephone: 555-1212   *Date Seen*: Month, day, year
                                         Psychologist: C. Linical, Ph.D.

Reason for Referral

Jessie was referred by her therapist at Community Mental Health
Center, Ms. Wanamaker, as well as at the request of P.
Sychiatrist, M.D. Dr. Sychiatrist requested information about
Jessie: specifically, whether she might be considered to display
borderline personality disorder. Ms. Wanamaker requested infor-
mation about possible treatment strategies.

Background Information

Ms. Wanamaker reports, in referring to Jessie, that "her whole motivation and values seem childishly punitive; people are liked by how much they do for her; grudges for fancied or real slights are cherished forever, revenge is a major goal; insulting or 'paying back' someone is prized and gloated over as a major achievement. Is there some therapeutic strategy to help make her a happier person?"

Assessment Results

Measures used:

Wechsler Adult Intelligence Scale–Revised (WAIS-R)
Bender Visual Motor Gestalt Test (Bender)
Woodcock-Johnson Psycho-Educational Battery (WJPEB; Reading cluster)
Beck Depression Inventory (BDI)
Minnesota Multiphasic Personality Inventory (MMPI)
Rorschach

Results of this assessment show that Ms. Smith displays many of the defining characteristics of borderline personality disorder: She shows a pattern of unstable and intense interpersonal relationships, inappropriate and unpredictable anger, identity disturbance, and affective instability. Other defining characteristics of borderline personality disorder (impulsivity in self-damaging behaviors, physically self-damaging acts, and chronic feelings of emptiness or boredom) were not observed or reported during this assessment, but may be present. The answer, then, to Dr. Sychiatrist's question as to whether Ms. Smith might appropriately be termed borderline is a tentative "yes."

Alternatively, but not mutually exclusive, aspects of her personality function to consider are her history of marriage to an abusive alcoholic and her combined, as Ms. Wanamaker reports it, "resentment and self-pity." Her ongoing attachment to an abusive man presents the possibility of dependent features in her personality functioning, and the types of difficulties she experiences in relationships with others suggest passive-aggressive behaviors.

All of these can coexist within the general rubric of borderline personality disorder; mixed features within a disorder are quite common, and it seems most likely that this is, in fact, what Ms. Smith presents.

Additional information that emerged from this assessment may be useful in working with Ms. Smith. Assessment of her general intellectual function indicates that she probably functions in the borderline range of general intellectual ability (WAIS-R Verbal IQ = 82; Performance IQ = 84; Full Scale IQ = 82). This level of ability implies that Ms. Smith may not be able to adapt in problematic life situations as easily as might higher-functioning persons. It also has implications for therapeutic strategy because it is unlikely that she will respond to verbal psychotherapy as readily or as positively as might a person who was functioning at higher levels in the verbal domain. This is not to say that verbal therapy with Ms. Smith is useless, but it does suggest that in working with her, vocabulary might be kept simple and that techniques that have concrete and observable aspects (such as behavioral self-recording) might be most successful with her.

Objective personality assessment (MMPI) indicates that Ms. Smith probably is experiencing levels of stress that lead her to feel a great need for support from others. Her profile suggests an exaggerated tendency to admit to personal problems, dysphoric mood, and many subjectively unusual experiences. Such a profile is often interpreted as a "cry for help," or an indication from the client that she feels an extremely strong need for psychological assistance. In such cases, establishing a positive therapeutic relationship can be a powerful factor in alleviating some more obvious symptomatology. The establishment of such a relationship with Ms. Smith, however, is likely to be complicated by her diminished capacity for mutuality in relationships as well as by her intense demands for gratification. A more thorough discussion of how to deal with the problem of relationship in psychotherapy with borderline clients is provided in the articles attached at the end of this report.

Ms. Smith's responses to the Beck Depression Inventory suggest the presence of severe depression. In the context of her overall personality structure, a history of suicidal attempts is likely, though not reported in referring her. If such a history has not been elicited, it is recommended that this issue be clarified with Ms. Smith. If antidepressant medications are used in the treatment of Ms. Smith, repeated administrations of the BDI could be helpful in charting the course of her response to medication and psychotherapy. Such repeat administrations could be accomplished easily by her staff therapist, if desired.

Ms. Smith's responses to the Rorschach suggest the possibility of impaired reality testing abilities. The content of her responses was often bizarre and morbid (for example, "a dead puppy cut up," "crabs and lobsters eating the flesh of a man"). In addition to being effectively determined distortions of her perception, these responses are consistent with severe depression and seriously impaired levels of ego function. A history of psychotic episodes is possible; here again, if this aspect of her background has not been clarified, it may be useful to do so.

Finally, as Ms. Smith is at present engaged in learning to read, I assessed her current reading skills. Although she reads at a fourth-grade level (equivalent to a percentile rank of 4 and a standard score of 74), she shows strengths in being able to reason about what she reads as a means of understanding it. It may be useful to monitor her progress in reading instruction and to support her in her efforts because this is one of the few areas in which she is making positive and successful efforts at improving her adaptive abilities.

Summary and Recommendations

Results of this assessment suggest that Ms. Smith presents many features of borderline personality disorder accompanied by dependent and passive-aggressive features. She indicates that she is extremely agitated and depressed at the present time; such extreme psychological disturbance may account for the reality testing difficulties noted. The possibility of a history of suicide attempts or overt psychotic symptomatology should be investigated if these issues have not been clarified already.

As a general therapeutic strategy, establishing a strong and positive, but judiciously intense therapeutic relationship can be expected to result in a reduction of some problems. Establishing realistic expectations for the therapeutic relationship, however, should also be emphasized. (See the articles attached for more specifics on this problem.)

Beyond this general strategy, a secondary goal should be to assist Ms. Smith in developing great adaptive abilities by teaching cognitive self-control techniques, developing appropriately assertive behavior, and increasing her social skills more generally. All these activities can enhance her capacity for operating more effectively in the world, and, at the same time, they will help her develop a more positive self-concept.

A potential limiting factor in Ms. Smith's development is her borderline level of intellectual function. As already noted, this factor should not be cause for undue pessimism, but should be taken into account in choice of therapeutic language and strategy. Techniques that stress concrete and observable activities are likely to be most successful with this client.

Diagnostic Impression

Axis I: Major Depression Disorder, Recurrent, Moderate Severity (DSM-IV 296.32)

Axis II: Borderline Personality Disorder (DSM-IV 301.83) with dependent and passive-aggressive features.

_____

Signature

Report III: Child Clinical/School

The next report illustrates the neuropsychological assessment of Tourette's Disorder with a child who has been manifesting attentional and behavioral difficulties in school. Notice that the psychologist who wrote the report has avoided a lengthy listing of tests administered, preferring to write them into the body of the report. This is one way neuropsychologists, who often administer in excess of 20 separate measures for an assessment, avoid taking up a large portion of the report with a simple listing of measures used. The lengthy Recommendations section of the report was included because it was to be transmitted to the school system in which the child was enrolled; in fact, it was made available to the school guidance counselor and school psychologist at a joint conference with the child's regular class teacher, tutor, and parent.

NEUROPSYCHOLOGY LABORATORY

Department of Neurology, University Hospital
Major American University, University Town, State
Name: West, Danny   *Hospital No.* 123456-7
Date: 5-18-95

Danny West is an 8-year, 10-month-old boy evaluated at the request of his mother, Ms. Linda West. Danny was diagnosed as having Tourette's Disorder in 1982 by pediatric specialists at the University Hospital, a diagnosis subsequently confirmed by Dr. A. K. Bernstein, an authority on Tourette's. Dr. Bernstein recommended that Danny receive a complete neuropsychological evaluation, and because of this recommendation, Ms. West contacted us. Danny's past medical history is unremarkable except for a severe illness (roseola) at age 9 months, when Ms. West reports he ran a fever of 106 degrees for approximately 5 days. Ms. West also reports, however, that she did not notice significant changes in Danny's behavior after this illness. Danny developed noticeable facial tics and throat clearing behaviors at about age 2 1/2 years.

Ms. West reports that Danny's tics are quite mild at present, and he has not been placed on Haldol. Significant present concerns are behavioral difficulties at school, including problems in getting along with classmates, completing work in school, and paying attention to his teacher. Our examiner reports that Danny indicated some displeasure with the length of testing (he had hoped to go to the zoo in the afternoon), but that once testing began, he was sufficiently cooperative for results of this evaluation to be considered valid. The examiner noted that Danny's attention varied with type of task and task length; in particular, it diminished with verbal tasks, which were difficult for him. She also reports that Danny responded well to praise for his efforts.

This assessment shows that Danny presents few of the neuropsychological deficits often reported to be associated with Tourette's Disorder. He probably functions in the average range of general intellectual ability and does not display the often-reported discrepancy between his performances on verbal versus visuospatial tasks (Wechsler Intelligence Scale for Children, 3rd Edition: Verbal IQ = 92; Performance IQ = 104; Full Scale IQ = 97). His performances on several measures of visuospatial problem solving (Raven's Matrices; Category Test) were slightly below average (consistent with others' reports of difficulties in this modality among children with Tourette's), but this finding is of equivocal significance in light of Danny's above-average performance on a measure of tactile-motor problem solving, also often below average among children with Tourette's (Tactual Performance Test).

As noted above, Danny's performance on a measure of general expressive verbal ability was average (Verbal IQ = 92), as was his performance on a measure of receptive vocabulary (Peabody Picture Vocabulary Test-Revised = 101). He also performed at grade level on a naming measure (Confrontation Naming subtest of the Clinical Evaluation of Language Function), but performed poorly on a measure of verbal learning (Verbal Paired Associates Test); he made errors that are consistent with the presence of learning difficulties. His pattern of errors on the verbal learning measure may also indicate the presence of linguistic difficulties. In light of this finding and the well-documented incidence of subtle language disturbances among children with learning and behavior difficulties, it is recommended that Danny receive a thorough language evaluation.

Assessment of Danny's academic skills suggests that current efforts in special education classes have been largely successful in helping him develop basic skills in reading and arithmetic. The academic goals outlined in his individualized educational plan for the 1991–1992 school year seem appropriate, and it appears unnecessary to add to them as a result of our evaluation.

Personality assessment through parent interview and report (Personality Inventory for Children) and interview with Danny indicate that he presents significant behavioral difficulties, which include a failure to develop age-appropriate social skills, attentional skills deficits, and, perhaps as a result of these difficulties coupled with problems in academic achievement, a negative self-concept. His present participation in a social skills group led by his elementary school counselor is completely appropriate and should continue. Other suggestions for dealing with Danny's behavior difficulties are included at the end of this report.

In summary, Danny presents few of the neuropsychological deficits often associated with Tourette's Disorder. There is some indication of minor difficulties in visuospatial problem solving, but this indication is of equivocal significance in light of his average performance on other measures that also tap this ability area. Danny probably has some difficulties in verbal learning consistent with problems in acquiring academic skills, but the special education interventions carried out with him thus far appear to have been quite successful. However, the possibility of subtle linguistic difficulties cannot be ruled out on the basis of this assessment, and a more thorough evaluation by a speech and language specialist is recommended. Such an evaluation is even more important in that a portion of Danny's social skills problems could stem from the types of linguistic difficulties known to occur among children with learning difficulties.

The following recommendations may be useful to those who are working with Danny:

1. It may be possible to improve Danny's attending by occasionally asking him, when his attention wanders, about what he's working on or how far he's progressed in the assignment. It is important in this situation to ask him to try to remember himself, as a preliminary step to his gradually acquiring the capacity to remind himself independently to return to work.

2 Danny may also be assisted in work-related behaviors by providing him with a cue to pay attention prior to giving directions or instruction. The adult who is working with

Danny might say something such as "Listen carefully," then pause, and when it is clear that Danny is attending, proceed with instruction.

3. Danny's ability to follow directions might also be strengthened by asking him to repeat directions after they are given. This process encourages him to pay close attention while he is being spoken to as well as ensuring that he knows the task to be done.

4. Danny may require frequent reminders to pay attention in class. He might be placed in the classroom near the teacher, who could arrange a nonverbal signal with him to remind him that he should pay attention. Such a nonverbal cue keeps the negative effects of teacher attention for inappropriate behavior to a minimum, but at the same time helps Danny attend appropriately to the task.

5. When demands for appropriate behavior or work performance are made on Danny, it is critical that they be enforced consistently. It is essential that Danny learn that there is no way for him to avoid behaving or performing according to the rules of the classroom. Related to this approach, it will be equally essential to provide him with praise when his behavior or performance meets the required standard.

6. When Danny's behavior is socially inappropriate, a strategy that might be helpful is to discuss his behavior and its results with him at a later date. A simple problem-solving strategy is to ask the following questions and encourage Danny to arrive at his own answers:
   a. "What happened that was a problem?"
   b. "How did you react?" or "What did you do?"
   c. "Is that how you want to react?"
   d. "How could you behave differently?"
   e. "Will you behave differently next time?"

7. Those who were working with Danny reported that when confronted with his misbehavior, he often denies that it occurred. In this situation, the denial should be treated as any other inappropriate behavior and targeted with a negative consequence. Arguments and discussions that

focus on Danny continuing to deny responsibility for his actions should be avoided, as the simple act of providing him attention for denial may make it more likely that he will deny other behavior in the future.

8. In working with Danny, it will probably be important to find and emphasize areas in which he can achieve success. Providing him with recognition in these areas may help him develop a more adequate sense of self-worth based on a realistic understanding that no one is good at everything and that having difficulty with academic tasks does not mean that he is a worthless person.

9. Danny should be encouraged to stop and think for a few moments before beginning a task in order to help him develop better planning skills. It may also be possible to help Danny develop better attending skills by encouraging him to remind himself to return to work when his attention wanders.

_____

Signature

Report IV: Forensic

The fourth report in this section illustrates how to respond to specific questions posed by legal authorities in assessing a person who has been adjudged not guilty by reason of insanity. This assessment took place about two years after the woman assessed committed a murder, and the court requested an opinion about whether she should be allowed a less restrictive placement and less supervision from the court and the community mental health center. Although the court transmitted its request with a series of overlapping and at times redundant questions, each question was addressed individually in the report.

PSYCHOLOGICAL REPORT

Name: Jane Jones
Address: 234 Somestreet,
Anytown, State
Telephone: 555-1234

Case No. 223344-0
DOB: Month, Day, Year
CA: 24
Date seen: Month, Day, Year
Psychologist: H. Schrink, Ph.D.

Reason for Referral

Ms. Jones was referred for evaluation by Judge V. Just of this county's Court of Common Pleas. Judge Just noted that Ms. Jones previously had been found not guilty by reason of insanity in a shooting incident in May of two years ago. Evaluation is requested at this time to determine whether Ms. Jones can be released to a less restrictive placement.

Background Information

Ms. Benjamin, a social worker for the court, provides the following information in referring Ms. Jones: "Client was found 'not guilty by reason of insanity' for the murder of a 55-year-old friend of her father 2 years ago. She was sent to the local state psychiatric facility from jail after she had been evaluated by a psychologist and a psychiatrist there. No previous psychiatric hospitalization or outpatient therapy is reported. Client stated at the time of the shooting that she shot the man in order to 'save' him because she had psychic experiences of him having sex with both males and females. She also stated that he propositioned her for sex . . . . She currently works at a sheltered workshop (she is ordered by the court to work there). She is functioning well in her job setting, although her counselor there notes that the client almost continually smiles or laughs by herself for no apparent reason."

Assessment Results

Sources of information

Minnesota Multiphasic Personality Inventory (MMPI)
Rorschach
Thematic Apperception Test (TAT)
Clinical Interview

Ms. Benjamin supplied a group of specific issues to be addressed in this evaluation:

1. Ms. Jones's capacity for repeating her offense
2. Her capacity for showing hostility
3. The nature of her relationships with peers
4. Her attitude toward authority, structured or otherwise
5. Her mental status
6. Her social outlook or attitudes
7. Her adaptation to the environment
8. Her social-emotional status

Capacity for repeating her offense. Results of this assessment show that Ms. Jones continues to show a number of behaviors and thought processes characteristic of schizophrenia. (Please see section below on her mental status.) The implication of this fact is that although her current behavior is neither violent nor hostile, the basic disorder (schizophrenia) that led to her offense continues to be present. It is apparent that her current status is due to her continuing psychiatric and vocational care rather than to a substantial change in her underlying disorder. Thus, the possibility that she might engage again in violent behaviors toward others cannot be ruled out, although it can be stated with reasonable certainty that she is unlikely to engage in such behavior if she continues to receive appropriate antipsychotic medication and remains in structured and supervised living and working situations.

Capacity for showing hostility. Careful review of Ms. Jones's record of contacts with her therapist at the community mental health center, as well as reports of her counselor at the sheltered workshop, does not show the recent occurrence of behaviors that indicate hostility toward herself or others. Ms. Jones's behavior during her interview with me, in which she was confronted on several occasions with facts she prefers not to acknowledge about her past behavior, did not lead her to become angry or hostile; in fact, she was quite well controlled. Thus, both her current reported behavior and her behavior during interviews suggest that she shows little overt hostility. She appears to have controlled her emotions rather rigidly so as to exclude the possibility of overt expression of anger or hostility.

Although this indicates a capacity for self-control, her rigid management of even the suggestion of irritation with others is a poor prognostic indicator because it shows that Ms. Jones probably has learned to deal with negative feelings by denying them rather than by acting on them adaptively. Thus, it is possible that outside of a controlled and supervised setting she might not be able to maintain this degree of control and might act on negative feelings about others.

Relationships with peers. Ms. Jones denies that she has emotionally significant relationships with others. She repeatedly stated that she preferred to spend her time by herself in order to read and study. A note in her therapist's record suggests that she may have some interest in relationships with men in that supervisors in the group home where she resides have noted that she has gone out in the evening to see men in the neighborhood. Both Ms. Jones's statements to me and her reported behavior suggest poor relationships with peers, which would not be a source of psychological support to her in stressful situations.

Attitudes toward authority. Although Ms. Jones clearly dislikes her supervised status, her attitudes expressed during my interview with her did not appear unreasonably hostile toward authority figures. It may be speculated that she has learned to deal with the legal and mental health systems by feigning compliance; it can be said that if this speculation is true, she has learned this lesson well.

Mental status. Ms. Jones was oriented to person, place, and time during my interview with her. Her affect was somewhat flattened, but otherwise was appropriate to her situation. She did not report hallucinations or delusions, nor did her behavior suggest that she was experiencing either. Her thought processes were illogical and rigid, and her principal way of dealing with any problem raised was to deny its existence. When confronted with her past behavior and its current consequences she blocked and became confused. Her mental status suggests that although her mental illness is well controlled by a combination of medical and rehabilitative interventions, it is still clearly present.

Adaptation to environment. In light of her limited psychological resources, Ms. Jones has made a good adaptation to her present environment. She has learned basic ways of dealing with others at work and in her living situation and has acquired the ability to deal with her closely supervised status without behaving inappropriately. Reports from her supervisors suggest that she performs well in a structured work setting. This pattern of adjustment indicates that continued placement in this sort of environment with very gradual loosening of restrictions at the court's discretion eventually may result in Ms. Jones's rehabilitation to a less closely supervised living situation.

Social-emotional status. Ms. Jones's overall status is thus typical of persons with controlled schizophrenia. Her long-term prognosis appears to be good with continued maintenance in a supervised setting and continued medication compliance. Ms. Jones's lack of insight into the nature of her illness, her failure to develop more adaptive ways of dealing with her emotions and with other persons, and her general reliance on denial as a way of dealing with topics she finds unpleasant all indicate that she will probably continue to require supervised living and working situations for the foreseeable future. In particular, it is reasonably likely that Ms. Jones might become noncompliant with her medication regime if she is not supervised. Should this occur, she is likely to become actively psychotic again. The consequences cannot be predicted accurately, but the possibility of violent behavior toward others cannot be ruled out. Thus, continued court supervision of Ms. Jones is indicated.

Summary and Recommendations

Results of this assessment show that Ms. Jones continues to manifest residual signs of schizophrenia even though she has made a good adjustment in supervised work and living settings. Although it is currently unlikely that she will display violent behaviors, the possibility of such behavior if she were to become noncompliant with her medications outside of her supervised setting cannot be ruled out. If she were to become actively psychotic, as might occur if she ceased to take the medications prescribed by her psychiatrist, her behavior is impossible to predict.

Therapeutic work with this client is likely to be an arduous and painstaking process. It will be very difficult to develop a positive and trusting relationship with her, although this sort of relationship is a necessary prerequisite to accomplishing meaningful change in psychotherapy with her. Extending unconditional positive regard for her as a person while gently and slowly confronting her on issues noted above about her emotional life and her interpersonal relationships is the psychotherapeutic approach most likely to be successful with her. A useful guide to working with clients similar to Ms. Jones is a text by Karon and Vandenbos, *Psychotherapy of Schizophrenia* (1981). Another useful work is Arieti's *Interpretation of Schizophrenia* (1974). These sources are recommended for specific therapeutic techniques with guarded and denying psychotic clients.

Diagnostic Impression

Axis I: Schizophrenia, Residual Type (DSM-IV 295.60)
Axis II: Schizotypal Personality Disorder (301.22)

_____

Signature

GLOSSARY

Causal link. *Causal links* establish a cause-effect relationship between certain elements in the report. They are critical in the relationship between conclusions and the referral question and between evaluations and recommendations. Whether a causal link exists can be tested by asking the question "Why?" For example, if the report includes answers to the referral questions and to why recommendations are made, then causal links exist.

Context. The *context* of the report comprises all aspects of the report's environment, including factors associated with the type of organization in which it functions and the type of person to whom it is directed.

Credible. The term *credible* is used in this book to indicate the capacity of the report *to change the beliefs or attitudes* of its readers. In studies of reports discussed in this book, participants were asked to use the term "credible" to refer to the extent to which a statement in a report led them to believe the assertion it contained.

Discourse comprehension. *Discourse comprehension* refers to the ability to understand interactive language. Although this usually refers to conversations among speakers, in this book several ideas are drawn from the research on discourse comprehension and applied to understanding the implicit conversation between reader and writer.

Expository Process Model. The *expository process model* specifies that certain relationships should exist between the elements of statements in reports. These include data, coordinating theoretical constructs, conclusions, and recommendations. Most broadly construed, the model provides report writers with guidance about how to make statements both *credible* and *persuasive*. See chapter 4 for a more complete explanation of the model.

Foreshadowing. *Foreshadowing* is the literary device by which the writer hints to the reader about what will follow. In the psychological report, for example, the writer may allude to a paragraph's conclusion in the way the opening sentence is constructed.

Format. Report *formats* discussed in this book describe the basic organization of report elements. Formats discussed include the letter and the brief or lengthy narrative reports, each with sections set off by headings.

Given-new contract. The *given-new contract* refers to the way in which speakers and listeners understand each other. In the psycholinguistic model discussed by Clark and Clark (1977), the given-new contract requires that the speaker provide unknown information (the *new*) about something with which the speaker and listener are both familiar (the *given*). In the sentence, "Mary hit the ball" the given element is "Mary" (who is presumably known to both the speaker and the listener), while "hit the ball" is the new element. The essence of this idea is that for speakers or writers to be understood by their audience, they must be certain that they all hold some information in common.

Middle-level construct. In discussion of psychological assessments, it is often useful or desirable to coordinate basic data, such as test scores or behavioral observations, with high-level conclusions through the use of explanatory terms such as *intelligence, anxiety,* or *psychosis*. These terms, lying as they do between low-level data and high-level conclusions, are called *middle-level constructs*.

Model. Reporting *models* refer to the ways in which assessment results are organized within report formats, whether test by test, by hypotheses about the meanings of test results for the referral questions, or by functional domains.

Persuasive. The term *persuasive* is used in this book to indicate the capacity of the report to change the behavior of its readers. In studies of reports discussed in this book, participants were asked to use the term "persuasive" to refer to the extent to which a statement in a report led them to act on the assertion it contained.

Psycholinguistic. *Psycholinguistic* refers to the psychological study of language. Currently, much of this study focuses on cognitive processes underlying language use.

Referral Problem Category System. A system of categories with which reasons for referral can be studies. (See Ownby, Wallbrown, D'Atri, & Armstrong, 1985, or Westman, Ownby, & Smith, 1987.)

Shared referents. This phrase denotes terms whose meanings are held in common by both speaker/writer and listener/reader. The given element in the given-new contract is typically a *shared referent*.

REFERENCES

Adams, K. M., & Heaton, R. K. (1985). Automated interpretation of neuropsychological test data. *Journal of Consulting and Clinical Psychology, 53,* 790–802.

Affleck, D., & Strider, F. (1971). Contribution of psychological reports to patient management. *Journal of Consulting and Clinical Psychology, 37,* 177–179.

American Psychological Association. (1981). Specialty guidelines for providers of psychological services. *American Psychologist, 36,* 640–681.

American Psychological Association. (1994). *Publication manual of the American Psychological Association* (4th ed.). Washington: Author.

Andrews, L. W., & Gutkin, T. B. (1991). The effects of human versus computer authorship on consumers' perceptions of psychological reports. *Computers in Human Behavior, 7,* 311–317.

Appelbaum, S. (1970). Science and persuasion in the psychological test report. *Journal of Consulting and Clinical Psychology, 35,* 349–355.

Arieti, S. (1974). *Interpretation of schizophrenia* (4th ed.). New York: Basic Books.

Bagnato, S. (1980). The efficacy of diagnostic reports as individualized guides to prescriptive goal planning. *Exceptional Children, 46,* 554–557.

Baker, H. (1965). Psychological services: From the school staff's point of view. *Journal of School Psychology, 3,* (4), 36–42.

Beck, A. T. (1976). *Cognitive therapy of the emotional disorders.* New York: International Universities Press.

Berry, K. K. (1975). Teacher impressions of psychological reports on children. *Journal of Pediatric Psychology, 3,* 11–14.

Binder, L. M. (1987). Appropriate reporting of Wechsler IQ and subtest scores in assessment for disability. *Journal of Clinical Psychology, 43,* 144–145.

Blau, T. H. (1991). *The psychological assessment of the child.* New York: John Wiley.

Brandt, H., & Giebink, J. (1968). Concreteness and congruence in psychologists' reports to teachers. *Psychology in the Schools, 5,* 87–89.

Brenner, C. (1957) Appendix: The reformulation of the theory of anxiety. In J. Rickman (Ed.), *A general selection from the works of Sigmund Freud* (pp. 236–246). New York: Doubleday.

Britton, B. K., & Black, J. B. (1985). Understanding expository text: From structure to process and world knowledge. In B. K. Britton & J. B. Black (Eds.), *Understanding expository text* (pp. 1–9). Hillsdale, NJ: Lawrence Erlbaum.

Brown, D. T. (1984). Automated assessment systems in school and clinical psychology: Present status and future directions. *School Psychology Review, 13,* 455–460.

Burke, M. J., & Normand, J. (1987). Computerized psychological testing: Overview and critique. *Professional Psychology: Research and Practice, 18,* 42–51.

Clark, H. H. (1985). Language use and language users. In G. Lindzey & E. Aronson (Eds.), *Handbook of social psychology* (3rd ed.), *Vol. II: Special fields and applications* (pp. 179–231). New York: Random House.

Clark, H. H., & Clark, E. V. (1977). *Psychology and language.* New York, Harcourt Brace Jovanovich.

Clark, H. H., & Haviland, S. E. (1977). Comprehension and the given-new contract. In R. O. Freedle (Ed.), *Discourse production and comprehension* (pp. 91–124). Norwood, NJ: Ablex.

Crimando, W., & Bordieri, J. E. (1991). Do computers make it better? Effects of source on students' perceptions of vocational evaluation report quality. *Rehabilitation Counseling Bulletin, 34,* 332–343.

Cuadra, C., & Albaugh, W. (1956). Sources of ambiguity in psychological reports. *Journal of Clinical Psychology, 12,* 267–272.

Dana, R. H., & Fouke, H. P. (1979). Barnum statements in reports of psychological assessment. *Psychological Reports, 44,* 1215–1221.

References

Dickson, D. H., & Kelly, I. W. (1985). The "Barnum effect" in personality assessment: A review of the literature. *Psychological Reports, 57,* 367–382.

Ellis, A., & Grieger, R. (1977). *Handbook of rational-emotive therapy.* New York: Springer.

Entin, E. E., & Klare, G. R. (1985). Relationships of measures of interest, prior knowledge, and readability to comprehension of expository passages. In B. A. Hutson (Ed.), *Advances in reading/language research* (Vol. 3, pp. 9–38). Greenwich, CT: JAI Press.

Forer, B. R. (1949). The fallacy of personal validation: A classroom demonstration of gullibility. *Journal of Abnormal and Social Psychology, 44,* 118–123.

Fowler, R. D. (1985). Landmarks in computer-assisted psychological assessment. *Journal of Consulting and Clinical Psychology, 53,* 748–759.

Gaddes, W. H. (1983). Applied educational neuropsychology: Theories and problems. *Journal of Learning Disabilities, 9,* 511–514.

Garfield, S., Heine, R., & Leventhal, M. (1954). An evaluation of psychological reports in a clinical setting. *Journal of Consulting and Clinical Psychology, 18,* 281–286.

Graham, J. R. (1982). *The MMPI: A practical guide* (2nd ed.). New York: Oxford University Press.

Gredler, G. (1987). [Review of *Psychological reports* by Raymond L. Ownby]. *Psychology in the Schools, 24,* 412–414.

Gregory, R. J. (1987). *Adult intellectual assessment.* Boston: Allyn & Bacon.

Hagborg, W. J. (1993). Parental understanding of their child's psychological evaluation findings conference. *Special Services in the Schools, 7,* 59–69.

Hanson, D. (1988). [Review of *Psychological reports* by Raymond L. Ownby]. *School Psychology Review, 17,* 522–524.

Harrower, M. (1965). Differential diagnosis. In B. B. Wolman (Ed.), *Handbook of clinical psychology* (pp. 381–402). New York: McGraw-Hill.

Hartlage, L., Freeman, W., Horine, L., & Walton, C. (1968). Decisional utility of psychological reports. *Journal of Clinical Psychology, 24,* 481–483.

Hartlage, L., & Merck, (1971). Increasing the relevance of psychological reports. *Journal of Clinical Psychology, 27*, 459–460.

Hartman, D. E. (1986). Artificial intelligence or artificial psychologist? Conceptual issues in clinical microcomputer use. *Professional Psychology: Research and Practice, 17*, 528–534.

Heidegger, M. (1949). *Existence and being.* Chicago: Henry Regnery.

Hollis, J. W., & Donn, P. A. (1979). *Psychological report writing: Theory and practice.* Muncie, IN: Accelerated Development.

Huber, J. T. (1961). *Report writing in psychology and psychiatry.* New York: Harper & Row.

Isett, R. & Roszkowski, M. (1979). Consumer preferences for psychological report contents in a residential school and center for the mentally retarded. *Psychology in the Schools, 16*, 402–407.

Jacob, S., & Brantley, J. C. (1987). Ethical-legal problems with computer use and suggestions for best practices: A national survey. *School Psychology Review, 16*, 69–77.

Karon, B. P., & Vanderbos, G. R. (1981). *Psychotherapy of schizophrenia.* New York: Aronson.

Keogh, B. (1971). Psychological evaluation of exceptional children: Old hang-ups and new directions. *Journal of School Psychology, 10*, 141–145.

Klopfer, W. G. (1960). *The psychological report: Use and communication of psychological findings.* New York: Grune & Stratton.

Kodimer, C. (1988). Neuropsychological assessment and Social Security disability: Writing meaningful reports and documentation. *Journal of Head Trauma Rehabilitation, 3*, 77–85.

Koffka, K. (1935). *Principles of gestalt psychology.* New York: Harcourt, Brace.

Kramer, J. J. (1988). Computer-based test interpretation in psycho-educational assessment: An initial appraisal. *Journal of School Psychology, 26*, 143–153.

Lacey, H., & Ross, A. (1964). Multidisciplinary views on psychological reports in child guidance clinics. *Journal of Clinical Psychology, 20*, 522–526.

Lacks, P., Horton, M., & Owen, J. (1969). A more meaningful and practical approach to psychological reports. *Journal of Clinical Psychology, 25*, 383–386.

References

Lerner, P. M. (1990). The clinical inference process and the role of theory. *Journal of Personality Assessment, 55,* 426–431.

Littlejohn, W. R. (1977). Judgments of three psychological report formats by school psychologists, teachers, principals, and school psychologist-educators. *Dissertation Abstracts International, 37,* 4992A–4993A. (Abstract).

McCullough, C. S., & Wenck, L. S. (1984). Current microcomputer applications in school psychology. *School Psychology Review, 13,* 429–439.

McGuire, W. J. (1985). Attitudes and attitude change. In G. Lindzey & E. Aronson (Eds.), *Handbook of social psychology* (3rd ed.), *Vol. II: Special fields and applications.* New York: Random House.

Marrow, A. J. (1969). *The practice theorist: The life and work of Kurt Lewin.* New York: Basic Books.

Matarazzo, J. D. (1983). Computerized psychological testing. *Science, 221,* 323.

Matarazzo, J. D. (1986). Computerized clinical psychological test interpretations. *American Psychologist, 41,* 14–24.

Mertens, D. M. (1976). Expectations of teachers-in-training: The influence of a student's sex and a behavioral vs. descriptive approach in a biased psychological report. *Journal of School Psychology, 14,* 223–229.

Millon, T., Green, C. J., & Meagher R. B. (1982). *Millon Adolescent Personality Inventory.* Minneapolis MN: National Computer Systems.

Moore, C., Boblitt, W., & Wildman, R. (1968). Psychiatric impressions of psychological reports. *Journal of Clinical Psychology, 24,* 373–376.

Mussman, M. (1964). Teachers' evaluations of psychological reports. *Journal of School Psychology, 3,* 35–37.

O'Dell, J. W. (1972). P. T. Barnum explores the computer. *Journal of Consulting and Clinical Psychology, 38,* 270–273.

Ownby, R. L. (1982). [Review of *Report writing in special education*]. *Psychology in the Schools, 19,* 576–578.

Ownby, R. L. (1984). The credibility and persuasiveness of psychological report statements derived from the expository process model (EPM). Unpublished data, Neuropsychology Laboratory, University of Wisconsin Hospital, Madison, WI.

Ownby, R. L. (1986a). The effects of certain variables on ratings of statements in psychological reports. Unpublished data, Kent State University.

Ownby, R. L. (1986b). *Manual for the referral problem category system, adult and child versions, experimental edition.* Unpublished manuscript available from author.

Ownby, R. L. (1990a). A study of the expository process model (EPM) with clinical and counseling psychologists. *Journal of Clinical Psychology, 40,* 366–371.

Ownby R. L. (1990b). A study of the expository process model in school psychological reports. *Psychology in the Schools, 27,* 353–358.

Ownby, R. L., & Matthews, C. G. (1985). On the meaning of the WISC-R third factor: Relations to selected neuropsychological measures. *Journal of Consulting and Clinical Psychology, 53,* 531–534.

Ownby, R. L., & Wallbrown, F. (1983). Evaluating school psychological reports, Part I: A procedure for systematic feedback. *Psychology in the Schools, 20,* 41–45.

Ownby, R. L., & Wallbrown, F. (1986). Improving report writing in school psychology. In T. Kratochwill (Ed.), *Advances in school psychology* (Vol. 5, pp. 7–49). Hillsdale, NJ: Lawrence Erlbaum.

Ownby, R. L., Wallbrown, F., & Brown, D. Y. (1982). Special education teachers' perceptions of reports written by school psychologists. *Perceptual and Motor Skills, 55,* 955–961.

Ownby, R. L., Wallbrown, F., & D'Atri, A. (1984). An analysis of referral problems for a four-year period. Unpublished data, Aurora City School District, Aurora, OH.

Ownby, R. L., Wallbrown, F., D'Atri, A., & Armstrong, B. (1985). The referral problems category system: A replication. *Special Services in the Schools, 1,* 53–66.

Palmer, J. (1970). *The psychological assessment of children.* New York: John Wiley.

Perls, F., Hefferline, R., & Goodman, P. (1951). *Gestalt therapy.* New York: Dell.

Petty, R. E., & Cacioppo, J. T. (1986). *Communication and persuasion.* New York: Springer.

Pryzwansky, W. B., & Hanania, J. S. (1986). Applying problem-solving approaches to school psychological reports. *Journal of School Psychology, 24,* 133–141.

Robinson, M. L. (1974). Psychological information to teachers and its effect on student achievement. *Dissertion Abstracts International, 34,* 4999A. (Abstract).

Rogers, C. (1961). *On becoming a person.* Boston: Houghton Mifflin.

Rosenthal, R., & Jacobson, L. (1968). *Pygmalion in the classroom.* New York: Holt, Rinehart & Winston.

Rubenzer, S. (1992). A comparison of traditional and computer generated psychological reports in an adolescent inpatient setting. *Journal of Clinical Psychology, 48,* 817–827.

Rucker, C. (1967a). Report writing in school psychology: A critical investigation. *Journal of School Psychology, 5,* 101–108.

Rucker, C. (1967b). Technical language in the school psychologist's report. *Psychology in the Schools, 4,* 146–150.

Sattler, J. (1974). *Assessment of children's intelligence.* Philadelphia: Saunders.

Sattler, J. (1982). *Assessment of children's intelligence and special abilities* (2nd ed.). Boston: Allyn & Bacon.

Sattler, J. (1988). *Assessment of children* (3rd ed.). San Diego, CA: Author.

Schwartz, E. B. (1977). Teacher perceptions of children as a consequence of differing content in psychological reports. *Dissertation Abstracts International, 39,* 584A. (Abstract).

Schwartz, N. H. (1987). Data integration and report writing. In Dean, R. S. (Ed.), *Introduction to assessing human intelligence* (pp. 289–313). Springfield IL: Charles C. Thomas.

Schwartz, N. H., & Wilkinson, W. K. (1987). Perceptual influence of psychoeducational reports. *Psychology in the Schools, 24,* 127–135.

Seagull, E. A. W. (1979). Writing the report of the psychological assessment of a child. *Journal of Child Clinical Psychology, 8,* 39–42.

Shea, V. (1985). Overview of the assessment process. In C. S. Newmark (Ed.), *Major psychological assessment instruments* (pp. 1–10). Boston: Allyn & Bacon.

Shively, J., & Smith, D. (1969). Understanding the psychological report. *Psychology in the Schools, 6,* 272–273.

Sinclair, E., & Alexson, J. (1986). Factor analysis and discriminant analysis of psychoeducational report contents. *Journal of School Psychology, 24,* 363–371.

Skinner, H. A., & Pakula, A. (1986). Challenge of computers in psychological assessment. *Professional Psychology: Research and Practice, 17,* 44–50.

Sloves, R. E., Docherty, E. M., & Schneider, K. C. (1979). A scientific problem-solving model of psychological assessment. *Professional Psychology, 10,* 28–35.

Smith, M. B. (1986). The plausible assessment report: A phrenological example. *Professional Psychology: Research and Practice, 17,* 294–295.

Sorrentino, P. (1985). Let's be technically right about technical writing. In B. Hutson (Ed.), *Advances in reading/language research* (Vol. 3 pp. 167–182). Greenwich, CT: JAI Press.

Strong, S. R. (1968). Counseling: An interpersonal influence theory. *Journal of Counseling Psychology, 15,* 215–224.

Strunk, W., Jr., & White, E. B. (1979). *The elements of style* (3rd ed.). New York: Macmillian.

Sudduth, R. S. (1976). The relative efficacy of three methods of presenting psychoeducational test data to teachers. *Dissertation Abstracts International, 36,* 7965A. (Abstract).

Sundberg, N. (1955). The acceptability of "fake" versus "bona fide" personality test interpretations. *Journal of Abnormal and Social Psychology, 50,* 145–147.

Sundberg, N. (1989). How to think and write about assessments [Review of *Psychological reports*]. *Contemporary Psychology, 34,* 66–67.

Sundberg, N., & Tyler, L. (1962). *Clinical psychology.* New York: Appleton-Century-Crofts.

Tallent, N. (1976). *Psychological report writing.* Englewood Cliffs, NJ: Prentice-Hall.

Tallent, N. (1980). *Report writing in special education.* Englewood Cliffs, NJ: Prentice-Hall.

Tallent, N., & Reiss, W. (1959a). Multidisciplinary views on the preparation of written clinical psychological reports: I. Spontaneous suggestions for content. *Journal of Clinical Psychology, 15,* 218–221.

Tallent, N., & Reiss, W. (1959b). Multidisciplinary views on the preparation of written clinical psychological reports: II. Acceptability of certain common content variables and styles of expression. *Journal of Clinical Psychology, 15,* 273–274.

Tallent, N., & Reiss, W. (1959c). Multidisciplinary views on the preparation of written clinical psychological reports: III. The trouble with psychological reports. *Journal of Clinical Psychology, 15,* 444–446.

Tanner, B. A. (1993). Computer-aided reporting of the results of mental retardation evaluations. *Behavior Research Methods, Instruments, and Computers, 25,* 203–207.

Tanner, B. A. (1994). The mental retardation report framework. *Behavior Research Methods, Instruments, and Computers, 26,* 213–214.

Taylor, J. L., & Teicher, A. (1946). A clinical approach to reporting psychological test data. *Journal of Clinical Psychology, 2,* 323–332.

Tedeschi, J. T., & Lindskold, S. (1976) *Social psychology.* New York: John Wiley.

Thomas, A. (1984). Issues and concerns for microcomputer uses in school psychology. *School Psychology Review, 13,* 469–472.

Walken, A. J. (Ed.). (1994). *Thesaurus of psychological index terms* (7th ed.). Washington, DC: American Psychological Association.

Walker, N. W., & Myrick, C. C. (1985). Ethical considerations in the use of computers in psychological testing and assessment. *Journal of School Psychology, 23,* 51–57.

Waugh, R. (1970). On reporting the findings of a diagnostic center. *Journal of Learning Disabilities, 3,* 629–634.

Weddig, R. R. (1984). Parental interpretation of psychoeducational reports. *Psychology in the Schools, 21,* 477–481.

Westman, J., Ownby, R. L., & Smith, S. (1987). An analysis of 180 children referred to a university hospital learning disabilities service. *Child Psychiatry and Human Development, 17,* 275–282.

Wiener, J. (1985). Teachers' comprehension of psychological reports. *Psychology in the Schools, 22,* 60–64.

Wiener, J. (1987). Factors affecting educators' comprehension of psychological reports. *Psychology in the Schools, 24,* 116–126.

Wiener, J., & Kohler, S. (1986). Parents' comprehension of psychological reports. *Psychology in the Schools, 23,* 265–269.

Wilkes-Gibbs, D., & Clark, H. H. (1992). Coordinating beliefs in conversation. *Journal of Memory and Language, 31,* 183–194.

Witt, J. C., Moe, G., Gutkin, T. B., & Andrews, L. (1984). The effect of saying the same thing in different ways: The problem of language and jargon in school-based consultation. *Journal of School Psychology, 22,* 361–367.

Woodford, F. P. (1967). Sounder thinking through clearer writing. *Science, 156,* 743–745.

Yalom, I. D. (1980). *Existential psychotherapy.* New York: Basic Books.

INDEX